ADVERSE POSSESSION

A practical legal guide

by

A. O. McCullough

Grosvenor House
Publishing Limited

The right of A. O. McCullough to be identified as the author of this
work has been asserted by him in accordance with Section 78
of the Copyright, Designs and Patents Act 1988

The book cover picture is copyright to Inmagine Corp LLC

This book is published by
Grosvenor House Publishing Ltd
28-30 High Street, Guildford, Surrey, GU1 3EL.
www.grosvenorhousepublishing.co.uk

A CIP record for this book
is available from the British Library

ISBN 978-1-78148-644-3

CONTENT

FOREWORD

'Adverse Possession' is commonly called 'Squatting.'

In more legal terminology Adverse Possession is the process used to describe a person living on and continually using property when that 'user' does not actually own or have any legal right to be doing so.

The purpose of this book is to illustrate the historical concept of Adverse Possession and why it was and remains necessary in modern social and legal contexts.

To then further address the practicalities of how and what makes a genuine Adverse Possession claim - or defence to such a claim - thereby arming any individual with a very strong theoretical and practical foundation in the topic.

To do so in a simple, easy to understand and logical manner.

- PLEASE NOTE -

This book was completed in the Spring of 2012 - all events, details etc, etc thereafter will obviously not be represented.

This book provides general and hopefully detailed guidelines
on the subject - however fully qualified professionals
should *always* be consulted in relation to *all*
aspects of Adverse Possession.

*The author accepts absolutely no responsibility whatsoever
for any completely unintentional errors that may be
contained within this book or
for any person/s who do not follow the above advice
on obtaining fully qualified legal advisors.*

SPECIALIST TERMINOLOGY

The history of Adverse Possession is extremely lengthy. Centuries of terminology (The meaning of a word or a phrase.) teamed with the adaptive uses of English words over this time frame have done little to improve the clarity of the situation.

Therefore for ease of use and consistency I have used the following self appointed terms -

'Paper owner' or 'Real owner' or 'True owner' or 'Legal owner'

To define that the property was/is actually owned by a person and that the act of Adverse Possession is against them.

'Squatter' or 'Adverse Possessor' or 'Possessor'

The term used to describe the person in Adverse Possession against the paper or true owner as defined above.

Property

'Land' or a 'Building - (House, flat, factory etc, etc.)'. or 'Land and a building or Buildings'

Limitation period

Is the term given to the time period required **_before_** an Adverse Possession claim can be made i.e. a 12 year limitation period would mean that 12 years of possession must pass **_before_** a claim can be made.

Please note - any other terms will be explained at the time.

CASE REFERENCES ETC

Case Referencing – offers the legal profession the opportunity to be (typically) awkward and confusing. For ease of appearance and reading I have merely stated the case and date - i.e. MR A v MR O (1972).

If the Case Reference 'code' is required the case will be listed alphabetically in the 'TABLE OF CASES' section of the book.

A similar list of the 'STATUTES' is also listed alphabetically in the 'TABLE OF STATUTES' section of the book.

All 'OTHER REFERENCES' made are also listed alphabetically in the 'OTHER REFERENCES' section of the book or noted at the time of use.

WHAT IS ADVERSE POSSESSION?

'Adverse Possession' in Northern Ireland, Wales and England or 'Perscription' in Scotland is the legal term used to describe the process by which a person can obtain legal ownership of what is, in effect, another person's property.

In Adverse Possession or Perscription cases the 'property' being discussed is always 'land and/or a building.'

The reason for the legal principle of Adverse Possession is explained in the '**POLICY OBJECTIVES**' section which follows.

('Private possessions' such as cars, electrics pets, etc, etc <u>are not</u> included within the topic of Adverse Possession/Prescription.)

1

UK REGIONAL VARIATIONS

From the outset it must be made clear that the majority of this book refers to England, Wales and Northern Ireland.

Scotland has drastically different procedures and rules for dealing with Adverse Possession. (Called Perscription) Indeed they are so drastic it would be fair to state Scotland has no true 'Adverse Possession' law but a system by which to settle 'garden border' disputes.

However to settle the 'garden border' disputes Scotland relies on the majority of Case Law reached in all UK Courts.

('Case Law' is the name given to Judge's rulings in previous Court Cases being applied to new and similar cases thereby establishing a stable and consistent system of judgements and clearly formulating what is - or is not - deemed good or bad evidence/legal practice etc.)

ENGLAND & WALES

Both regions are covered by THE LIMITATION ACT (1980) for all **unregistered** land. (It also includes **registered** land where 12 + years Adverse Possession has been obtained before 25th February 2002) and

THE LAND REGISTRATION ACT (2002) (for **registered** land.)

To obtain a favourable Adverse Possession Judgement a person must occupy the property (Land and/or a building) for -

1)   A continual period of time required by the law. (Called the 'limitation period'.)

and

2)   Do 1 (above) in a certain way, which is also required by the Courts. (Providing evidence which displays 'individual,' 'continual' and 'effective control' of a 'fixed area'.)

If a person achieves both these conditions they may be entitled to become the legal owner of the property (Land and/or building.)

In Wales & England the main legislation for the legal time frames (Limitation periods) and processes required to claim Adverse Possession are currently contained in –

1)   For property (Land and/or buildings) **unregistered** at the Land Registry – The LIMITATION ACT (1980) - which sets a limit of 12 years or more before a claim for Adverse Possession will be entrained. (This Act also includes **registered** land

where 12 + years Adverse Possession has been obtained before 25th February 2002.)

2) For property (Land and/or buildings) **registered** at the Land Registry – THE LAND REGISTRATION ACT (2002) - which establishes a slightly more complex approach. Here a 10 year limit for such a claim is required. These 10 years may be enough – if no one protests the claim - but can be followed by a further 2 years 'waiting period.' (Totalling 12 years) before an Adverse Possession claim will be recognised.

LAND REGISTER OF ENGLAND & WALES

The LAND REGISTRY ACT (1862) and LAND TRANSFER ACT (1875) provided for voluntary registration of title deeds. By 1897 THE LAND TRANSFER ACT (1897) made registration compulsory for regions which opted to adopt such a process – London did so and by 1990 all regions had.

The register holds some 20 million titles (Three trillion pounds worth.) Some 90% of buildings are registered and about 50% of land is registered.

The land registry has 'physical offices' and a 'web' or 'mail' presence. (See below.)

Searches on properties can currently be arranged for about £2.00 for an online or in person 'search' or by post for around £4.00.

You will need the postal address and/or accurate details of the location you wish to examine.

There are 24 Land Registry offices spread throughout England and Wales. The Head office is located at –

34 Lincolns Inn Fields
London
WC2A 3PH
Tel: 0800 432 0432
E mail - registerland@landregistry.gsi.gov.uk
Web - landregistry.gov.uk

The 24 Regional Offices, each responsible for a distinct geographic area, are at Birkenhead (Old Market), Birkenhead (Rosebrae), Coventry, Croydon, Durham (Boldon), Durham (Southfield), Gloucester, Harrow, Kingston upon Hull, Leicester, Lytham St Anne's, Lancashire Office (also based at Lytham St Anne's), Nottingham East, Nottingham West, Peterborough, Plymouth, Portsmouth, Stevenage, Swansea (covering all of Wales), Telford, Tunbridge Wells, Weymouth and York.

NORTHERN IRELAND

This region of the UK is covered by the LIMITATION ACT (1980) via the Statutory Instrument 1989 No. 1339 (N.I. 11) (THE LIMITATION NORTHERN IRELAND ORDER 1989.) for both **unregistered** and **registered** land

Northern Ireland is <u>not</u> covered by the LAND REGISTRATION ACT (2002)

To obtain a favourable Adverse Possession Judgement a person must occupy the property (Land and/or a building) for -

1) A continual period of time required by the law. (Called the 'limitation period'.)

And

2) Do 1 (above) in a certain way - which is required by the Courts. (Providing evidence which displays 'individual,' 'continual' and 'effective control' of a 'fixed area'.)

If a person achieves both these conditions they may be entitled to become the legal owner of the property (Land and/or building.)

For property (Land and/or buildings) **registered** or **unregistered** at the Land Registry – The Northern Irish variation of the LIMITATION ACT (1980) - sets a limitation period of 12 years or more before a claim for Adverse Possession will be entrained.

LAND REGISTER OF NORTHERN IRELAND
(Part of - 'Northern Ireland Land & Property Services')
Lincoln Building
27 – 45 Great Victoria Street
Belfast
BT2 7SL
Tel - 028 902 51700
Web - lrni.gov.uk

From as early as 1708 a system called 'Memorial' registration was in voluntary action. THE LAND REGISTRATION ACT (2002) made it compulsory throughout the region.

The registry states that it has no accurate figures but it estimates registered property amounts to about 60 – 70% of all buildings and about 90% of all land.

Searches on properties can currently be arranged for about £2.00 for an online or in person 'search' or by post for around £4.00.

You will need the postal address and/or accurate details of the location you wish to examine.

SCOTLAND

Scotland - in effect - does not have 'Adverse Possession.' It operates a system called 'Prescription.' THE PRESCRIPTION AND LIMITATION (SCOTLAND) ACT (1973) contains the 'Scottish system' of Adverse Possession.

Please note - The limitation period in Scotland is set at 10 years.

Under the principles of Prescription a person in possession is not considered as the owner unless he/she can combine this possession with some link to 'paper title' i.e. the deeds.

Therefore possession being adverse to the true owners paper title or the length of the time the possession was held for is not in the least important if a person cannot tie these factors to some form of 'paper entitlement.'

Due to this procedure Scottish law is wholly concerned with (and limited to) the interpretation of deeds/maps and physical 'garden border' or historical disputes.

If your deeds indicate you could possibly own the property in dispute AND you have been acting as said possessor you may be entitled to have yourself declared official 'paper owner' at the Land Registry.

The Case Law used to determine such possession is largely identical for other regions of the UK.

('Case Law' is the name given to Judge's rulings in previous Court Cases being applied to new and similar cases thereby establishing a stable and consistent system of judgements and clearly formulating what is - or is not - deemed good or bad evidence/legal practice etc.)

Therefore the only time 'Adverse Possession' law - as applied in the rest of the UK - becomes relevant in Scotland is when the conditions of Prescription are meet and Case Law – applied elsewhere in the UK - is used to settle the dispute.

It is for this reason that the majority of this book is England, Northern Ireland and Wales centred and Scotland has largely been isolated to its own section with links to other topics throughout the book - please bear this in mind.

Land registration in Scotland (THE LAND REGISTER (SCOTLAND) ACT (1979)) began the process of county-by-county compulsory registration of all new land transfers, inheritances, sales etc. By 2003 the ACT applied in all counties. Currently some 53% of buildings and only 10% of land is registered.

The 'Keeper' (Register of Scotland) does; "not compile figures or keep a log for the number of applications…" which could be classed as Adverse Possession.

<u>REGISTER OF SCOTLAND</u>

153 London Road
Edinburgh
EH8 7AU
Telephone – 0131 659 6111
Fax – 0131 479 3688
Email - keeper@ros.gov.uk
Web – www.ros.gov.uk

24 Douglas Street
Glasgow
G2 7NQ
Telephone – 0141 306 1500
Fax – 0141 306 1505

Searches on properties can currently be arranged for about £2.00 for an online or in person 'search' or by post for around £4.00

You will need the postal address or accurate details of the location you wish to examine.

ADVERSE POSSESSION POLICY OBJECTIVES 'USE IT OR LOSE IT'

Put in its most basic terms – property (Land and/or Building/s) is a valuable commodity and prized resource. The waste of such by a person for whatever reason should never be valued or encouraged over the use of it - even by another person.

In the UNITED STATES OF AMERICA case of WARSAW V CHICAGO METALIC CEILINGS INC (1985) this emotion was very clearly stated – the public and public bodies have historically favoured use over disuse and the law therefore prefers a person who uses the land over an owner who does not. It prefers this to the point where it will go to the lengths to provide a legal process by which it can strip the absentee paper owner of his or her rights (and property) and hand them to the user of the property.

The 'policy' is simply there to encourage the efficient use of property (Land and Buildings). It really is a case of - 'use it or lose it.'

UNITED NATIONS
No less than the UNITED NATIONS (UN) -
(CENTRE FOR HUMAN SETTLEMENTS FOR THE

IMPROVEMENT OF LAND REGISTRATION AND LAND INFORMATION IN THE DEVELOPING COUNTRIES (UNCHS NAIROBI 1990) poured scorn on 'absentee land owners' over land which could be used to a fuller potential. The UN even called for every nation to set up and encourage a vigorous, cheap and easy to use Adverse Possession legal procedure as a vital tool to ensure such 'use' became the norm.

EUROPEAN UNION
The European Courts (Whose judgements are currently enforceable in the UK Courts.) also agreed with the UN. In its own ruling in the PYE (JA) (OXFORD) V GRAHAM (2000 & 2007) case it even stated that the UK's 12-year limitation period was; "...long." (At paragraph 38) and "...relatively long." (At paragraph 69) It went on to clearly state that distinguishing between registered or unregistered land should make no difference to this concept suggesting that the UK was awkward toward Adverse Possessors for no valid reason.

UNITED KINGDOM
UK policy on Adverse Possession (As the European Courts noted.) is a contradictory business the naked hostility from the legal profession is long running. In 'ancient times' of kings, lords, knights and bishops the desire was to ensure that said kings, lords, knights and bishops could behave as they pleased whilst their interests were protected by puppet Courts of State. However common sense and 'commoners' disputes resulted in a body of Case Law developing around the fringes of the topic where kings, lords, knights

and bishops were unaffected – in short Adverse Possession law developed as it was necessary. It continued to grow.

Kings, lords and knights gave way to politicians and an increasingly secular, capitalist society; the fringes of Adverse Possession law grew quietly towards the centre. However the Courts hostility still lingers on in the attitude of the legal professions desire to protect 'paper owners.'

It must be remembered that certain Judges, especially higher ranking Judges are either titled gentry or 'wannabe gentry' who move in certain social circles. They are not inclined to be warm to 'squatters' and whist victory in higher Courts i.e. the COURT OF APPEAL may be more likely as the law is more rigidly applied, the cost of such an appeal will run into the tens, if not hundreds of thousands of pounds and a frightening amount of time and physical stress.

It must be remembered that Judges have the ability to use their own 'discretion' to distinguish your case if they so desire – in short - a glance at any 'honest' legal case book shows - they can crush a case on an arguably 'half baked' notion, a mere play on words or twist of facts which suits their own mindset rather than what is strictly legally justified.

For example In CAVE V ROBINSON JARVIS AND ROLF (2002) it was noted that from THE LIMITATION ACT (1623) and for some 400 years hence 'Adverse Possession' was Statue based. Knowing this, one would suspect that the law should therefore be rather 'formulised' on this topic.

However arguments over the meaning of 'Adverse,' over the meaning of 'Possession' and over 'registered land' and 'unregistered land'. Debate over the intention of the squatter and endless other additional issues have endlessly been allowed to reoccur over these 400 years with some judges showing no desire to standardise the situation to any degree of certainty.

Thus the UK Courts and political system seem to feel cursed with the notion of Adverse Possession and yet charmed and railroaded by its practicality - Keeping property in use is simply very good public policy.

Despite the twisted behaviour of the UK Courts - the CHOLMONDELEY V CLINTON CASE (1817 & 1820) had them state that a person in long time 'possession' should legally be left to such. In MANBY v BEWICKE (1857) it was ruled such an approach was 'civilised.'

150 years later a report by the LAW COMMISSION (NO. 271 PARAGRAPH 2.72 (1998)) - which led to the LAND REGISTRATION ACT (2002) – it was repeated that land continued to be a "...precious resource and should be kept in use and in commerce."

They need Adverse Possession – they just don't like it very much!

CURRENT USAGE RATES OF ADVERSE POSSESSION & LEGAL COVERAGE/ ATTITUDE TO THE TOPIC

Adverse Possession must be popular – It has appeared in 'The Simpson's' episode 'Bart Carny' (12th episode of 'The Simpson's' 9th season) where Cooder and Spud - a travelling carnival, single parent family wish to thank the Simpson family for providing them with temporary lodgings. Cooder buys his hosts tickets for a day trip on a glass bottom boat. The Simpson's return from their brief trip to find the house locks changed and Cooder 'the squatter' claiming ownership of their home. Homer and family are forced to live in the tree house where they plan revenge, which mostly revolves around a house fire whilst Cooder and Spud sleep.

A Fine example of 'parasitic squatting' – invading a family's home and a mile away from what 'civilised squatting' – the responsible use of what no one else seems to want.

More statistically, during the passage of THE LAND REGISTRATION BILL (2002) through parliament it was noted that the Land Registry receives <u>over</u> 20,000 applications for registration based on Adverse Possession per year. (This figure is certainly considerably lower than it should be as it only includes Wales and England as Northern Ireland and Scotland do not hold such details.)

The Registered Institute of Chartered Surveyors (RICS) web site also concludes that the Land Registry deals with at least 1,350 claims a month.

MARK WONNACOTT in his book 'POSSESSION OF LAND' (2006) puts it less statistically but more eloquently – "Every week in county courts up and down the country, there are people spending £50,000 or more, fighting domestic boundary disputes, typically over six inches of residential back-garden and counting the money well spent if the judge decides that the boundary is where they say it should be" (Page ix)

It can also be noted that despite the counter intuitive hype happily spread by certain dominate parties in the legal sector that in 15,000 (75%) of these cases it is the squatter who becomes the successful party.

These 'squatters' are in good company. The United Nations, European Courts and UK Courts have supported Adverse Possession.

The Queen herself (Crown) in ROBERTS (MARK ANDREW) V CROWN ESTATE COMMISSIONERS (2008) won legal ownership after 'squatting' on lands worth millions at the Severn Estuary under the paper ownership of Mark Andrew Tudor. (Who likes to use the 'pompous ass' title 'Lord Marcher of Trelleck.')

'The squatter in Buckingham Palace' case should leave the reader in no doubt of the reality of Adverse Possession or the variety of people who avail of it.

Adverse Possession is therefore an extremely relevant and common feature in the UK's legal landscape.

However if one goes to the World Wide Web and selects their search engine of choice. Takes themselves to any of our UK libraries and makes proper use of their extremely extensive 'book search' facilities. If one turns up at any main street booksellers and again uses their extensive book search facilities you will quickly come to a realisation – legal professionals do not want to talk about such a subject. The legal professionals do not want to talk about 'that little topic' at all.

Such a common and relevant subject. A subject with at least 20,000 and counting cases per annum and the number of textbooks, manuals or detailed explanatory references amounts to next to nothing - At best a handful of web sites glibly brush upon the topic, a few Land Law books pay a few pages of attention to it. Indeed one would be very hard pressed to think of any other such 'high usage' subject that receives so much under representation.

So what will you find in these extensive searches – you will find one single, solitary book (with 2 editions) on the topic – 'Adverse Possession' by 'Stephen Jourdan' 1st edition published by 'Butterworths LexisNexis' in 2003 (ISBN 0 406 98251 1) 2nd edition published by 'Bloomsbury Professional' by Stephen Jourdan

QC & Oliver Radley-Gardner, published 2011 (ISBN 978 1 84766 372 6)

Both are priced at a ridiculous amount - second hand copies sell for around £200+ on '<u>amazon.com</u>' – This price and it's written in that lofty regal twang only legal professionals use. It is arguably not for any but the most determined 'human' person. It is far from easy reading and like most legal documentation is in no sensible arrangement other than the arrangement that confuses any sane person but lets legal professionals hand us such very big bills for pretending they actually do understand it –

If you cannot explain a thing concisely, you do not understand it yourself!

So be under no illusion - The legal profession and anything that flutters around it sees little profit in publishing laws the public – who must abide by them - can actually understand. As my father would put it more precisely - "For God's sake they still use Latin." (I do not know if he meant they still actually use the Latin language or if it all sounded like Latin even when in the 'English' language – but he most likely meant both.)

In Mr Jourdan's (and later Mr Radley Gardner's) defence they did have the great courage to write the book. I also assume Mr Jourdan's 1st edition was written exclusively for legal professionals. It has certainly been used as an authority/reference point by judges in actual legal cases and it was completely indispensible to my own research.

Many of its extracts, in the hands of a determined human being i.e. not a legal professional - whatever species they may be - are relevant and somewhat understandable. Unfortunately, in my humble opinion, most will have little time for Mr Jourdan's effort - 80% of the some 700 pages need never have been written. It is heavy going and the usual lengthy verbal diarrhoea of legal professionals has unfortunately dominated.

The above points are raised, not to upset Mr Jourdan and his professional chums – they wrote what they set out to write - but to illustrate that if any person decides to research Adverse Possession or bring such a case they will not be treated warmly by prevailing legal forces which make the task as daunting and awkward as they possibly can – do not be afraid – good legal advisors and determination result in a 75% success rate for the squatter.

HISTORY

In practical terms one need never read the following 'historical' chapters but they provide a background for those with a more educational interest in the subject.

Please remember that, in the main, this history follows Wales, Northern Ireland and England as Scotland has adopted a slightly different procedure (As explained previously.)

PRE 1833

The law of what we now call 'Adverse Possession' could best be described by the 'unknown students' impolite scribble in the left hand margin of Stephen Jourdan's 1st edition of his Adverse Possession book - "What the f**k???"

In the main Medieval law on the topic was highly complex and largely, if not totally, dependant upon what the Judge felt like ruling – hence a difficulty in rationally explaining the rules of the game at all.

By 1623 such 'real actions' or 'seisen' had raised many eyebrows and the LIMITATION ACT (1623) (aka THE STATUTE OF JAMES) was introduced to set a 20-year limit for Adverse Possession claims (Limit did not apply to Crown property. Crown land was governed by the CROWN SUITS ACT (1769), amended by the CROWN SUITS ACT (1861) and then covered by the LIMITATION ACT (1939))

This 1623 ACT, in the main was to prevent Judges from making up 'on the spot' time limits and elements of evidence as they had previously been doing on a case-to-case basis. (Please note this is a trend they still have not properly rid themselves of.)

The Courts/Judges form the outset took a dislike to the 1623 ACT and 'defined' it to re-inject confusion – Adverse Possession was contorted to mean 'a use' the real owner would not have applied to the property. An inquiry would be used to establish if there was such a possession and soon a complex maze of Judge 'invented' rules and demands for what ever evidence a Judge felt like demanding or ignoring began to infest the topic yet again. In particular the tools of implied consent/license at will were used to make the possession 'consensual' but were "Simply invented [ways] to prevent possessions from being adverse." (Page 24 2nd ed. Adverse Possession Jourdan & Radley-Gardner)

By 1829 the topic had become such a cess pit that the FIRST REPORT OF THE COMMISSIONERS ON THE LAW OF REAL PROPERTY stated the system was nothing more than "...very unsystematic and very defective." They drew up new proposals in the shape of THE REAL PROPERTY LIMITATION ACT (1833)

Thus, with glee, it can be pointed out that 'seisen' or 'real actions' and the LIMITATION ACT (1623) are no longer of any relevance or importance whatsoever to the modern topic. Only the legal professions 'odd' attitude towards Squatters has lingered on.

POST 1833

THE REAL PROPERTY LIMITATION ACT (1833) **(also referred to as THE LIMITATION ACT** (1833)) abolished the above STATUTE OF JAMES (1623) on 24 July 1833 and the 'new age' of Adverse Possession began.

This point was underlined four years later in the case of NEPEAN V DOE D KNIGHT (1837) when the COURT OF THE EXCHEQUER CHAMBER deemed arguments made under anything but the new 1833 ACT were wholly irrelevant.

The case also, thankfully, retired the concept of 'Adverse Possession' meaning the squatter must use the land in a way adverse to the true owners use of the land to the history books; "…the right accrued whatever be the nature of the possession."

It is very important that you remember the decision in the NEPEAN V DOE D KNIGHT (1837) case for reasons that will soon become very, very clear.

With regards to this ruling also see - some of the many, many - supporting cases of –

CULLEY v DOE D TAYLERSON (1840) (At 1015) JACK V WALSH (1842)

SMITH V LLOYD (1854)
MAGDALEN HOSPITAL V KNOTTS (1878)
JOLLY GATHERCOLE V NORFOLK (1900)
PARADISE BEACH AND TRANSPORTATION CO
LTD V PRICE ROBINSON (1968)
PYE (JA) (OXFORD) LTD V GRAHAM (2000) (see
UKHL 30 (2002) 3 WLR 221 PARAGRAPH 33 – 35)
&
TRELOAR V NUTE (1977) where it was again ruled
ridiculous to argue possession depended on having to
'annoy' the real owner in some manner. No authority
has ever been established to cite such. This would
simply allow the paper owner to say he/she was not
annoyed to win any such claim against them.

"Indeed if inconvenience to the owner had to be
established it would be difficult ever to acquire a ...
title since the owner if inconvenienced would be likely
to take proceedings."

(Perversely this 'annoyance' is now exactly the
opportunity the LAND REGISTRATION ACT (2002)
provides for registered property owners in England and
Wales.)

Thus in PYE V GRAHAM (2007) the Judges clearly
stated that it was simply - "Heretical and wrong."
(Para 45) to try and reintroduce such a contorted
notion of 'adverse' as regards possession. They pointed
out it was now well established that possession
depended on control of an area and intention to retain
such control regardless of how the possession was
conducted.

(Many of the 1833 ACTS provisions still survive to this day and have passed into newer ACTS such as THE LIMITATIONS ACT (1939) and LIMITATION ACT (1980).)

THE REAL PROPERTY LIMITATION ACT (1874) became law on 7 August 1874 and pretty much left in force the 1833 ACT except for one very important change - the limitation period for claiming possession was brought down from 20 years to 12 years.

LAW OF PROPERTY ACT (1925) also did little to alter the original 1833 Act.

THE LIMITATION ACT (1939)
The FIFTH INTERIM REPORT OF THE LAW REVISION COMMITTEE (1936) published a report of recommendations which were implemented in THE LIMITATION ACT (1939) - a so-called 'consolidation act' to 'clarify' the previous collection of ACTS - Or glowing testimony that the Committee had been working harder on lunch than on the question at hand.

It also reintroduced the term 'Adverse Possession.' and defined the new meaning at SECTION 10(1) to mean – "…possession of some person in whose favour the period of limitation can run." Thus underlining – in statute (law) - its post 1833 meaning of 'Adverse Possession' as set out in NEPEAN V DOE D KNIGHT (1837).

This definition has been underlined relentlessly - most notably in the PYE (JA) (OXFORD) GRAHAM (2000) case (At UKHL 30 (2002) 3 WLR 221 at paragraph 35 – 36) -

(At paragraph 35) – "...not a [reintroduction] by a side wind after over 100 years the old notion of Adverse Possession in force before 1833." and "...must not be allowed to re-introduce by the back door that which for so long has not formed part of the law."

(At Paragraph 36) "The question is simply whether the defendant squatter has dispossessed the paper owner by going into ordinary possession of the land for the requisite period without the consent of the owner." It was not about being 'adverse' to what the paper owner might have done.

The 1939 ACT also introduced new time limitation periods for Crown land – 30 years. Foreshore – 60 years. Spiritual or eleemosynary corporations - 30 years. (Discussed later.)

New rules on fraud, concealment and disability were introduced or modified allowing the extension of the limitation period to cover such cases. (Discussed later.)

CURRENT LAW

LIMITATION ACT 1980

The 21ST REPORT OF THE LAW REFORM COMMITTEE (1977) led to the LIMITATION ACT (1980), yet another 'more hard work on the lunch' than hard work on the law. This 'consolidation act' largely supplemented no real change and confirmed the limitation periods were appropriate.

As WONNACOTT would state – "No one sitting down with a blank piece of paper, attempting to produce a rational & coherent property – law code, would produce that which the forces of history... have produced in England and Wales... That nonetheless is what we have." (Page 91)

THE LIMITATION ACT (1980) is still currently in force in England and Wales for all **unregistered** land (and **registered** land where more than 12 years Adverse Possession has elapsed before 25 February 2002)

It applies to all **registered** or **unregistered** land in Northern Ireland.

I, again, remind the reader that Scotland operates a different procedure and this ACT has no relevance in Scotland.

THE LAND REGISTRATION ACT (2002)

The LAW COMMISSION published the REPORT ON LIMITATION OF ACTIONS in (2001) – this time it appeared they had, in a completely perverse way, worked for their lunch and the legal professions hostility to Adverse Possession in the face of common sense had been reinvigorated from a different direction.

THE LAND REGISTRATION ACT (2002) is still currently in force in the UK regions of England and Wales for registered land.

This ACT is not relevant to either Northern Ireland or Scotland.

In Scotland **THE LAND REGISTER (SCOTLAND) ACT (1979)** is the current relevant legislation.

THE HUMAN RIGHTS ACT 1998

This ACT came into force in the UK in 2 October 2000 giving direct legal effect of the EUROPEAN CONVENTION FOR THE PROTECTION OF HUMAN RIGHTS AND FUNDAMENTAL FREEDOMS - (ECHR).

In short the laws the UK Government makes must comply with ECHR law. If it does not it can be 'struck out.' i.e. declared illegal by UK Judges who are legally required to ignore the intentions of a freely elected, sovereign, UK parliament and enforce European Law. UK Judges will continue to do so unless the UK Parliament passes an ACT telling them not to.

Legal professional types leapt on the HUMAN RIGHTS ACT (1988) as the end of Adverse Possession. The relentless and unfounded hype was that THE FIRST PROTOCOL ARTICLE 1 of the ECHR – the right to peacefully enjoy ones possessions - would kill all such claims stone dead. These legal types quickly flustered up a real storm in a teacup over Adverse Possessions demise. However Adverse Possession is a very practical fellow, heavily armoured with a great deal of common sense.

The Protocol protects rights – but whose rights – the rights of property owners to be absentee landlords or the rights of those who – after centuries of history and public policy the world over had used the land productively?

In light of the ECHR, FIRST PROTOCOL, ARTICLE 1 The PYE (JA) (OXFORD) LTD V GRAHAM (2000) case became the legal professionals 'sexy poster boy' - the 'big gun' that would soon put the final shot into Adverse Possession over the right to peacefully enjoy ones possessions without the complications Adverse Possessors entail.

After numerous appeals from one Court to a higher Court the PYE (JA) Case finally entered the highest chamber in the European Court and far from the outcome the legal 'in crowd' where gleefully advertising – public policy, hundreds of years of global history and pure common sense insured Adverse Possession was still smiling and safely walked intact from the chamber.

Adverse Possession was given a clean bill of health. PYE (JA) (OXFORD) V GRAHAM (2000) might have been a smoking gun but Adverse Possession proved very bullet proof and fighting fit for purpose in the 21st century.

Property was not to be left idle and after due legal process with a set limitation period, (As established by Government.) the right of any person – who was in actual physical possession - was deemed a superior 'right to peaceful possession' than that of some 'paper owner' who had abandoned possession long ago.

The PYE case was quickly underscored by OFULUE (EMMANUALE) & AGNES OFULUE V BOSSERT (ERICA) (2008) where the European Court sitting in Strasburg again found its ruling in PYE (JA) (OXFORD) V GRAHAM (2000) was just.

The PYE (JA) (OXFORD) V GRAHAM (2000) case was decided before the LAND REGISTRATION ACT (2002)

The procedure/rules for claiming Adverse Possession on registered land have now altered dramatically due to that ACT which provides a procedure which, many would argue, has the major intent of over protecting absentee property owners. It also seems to protect the UK Government from a disposed owner making a financial claim for compensation against said Government.

This protection does not seem prudent for THE LAND REGISTRATION ACT (2002) desperately attempts to protect 'registered land' and 'true owners' for no good public policy reasons. The most glaring dichotomy is that unregistered property claims and the evidence required for registered property claims remain identical as embodied in the LIMITATION ACT (1980) and the surrounding Case Law.

The PYE (JA) (OXFORD) V GRAHAM (2000) ruling in the European Courts even gave UK LIMITATION ACT (1980) and its application a clean bill of health and merely stated that if a paper owner who had lost an Adverse Possession case brought action against the UK Government on the grounds that they were not compensated for their loss of property this case would '*perhaps*' be welcomed at the European Court and a decision to oblige national Government to compensate dispossessed paper owners '*might*' be considered.

In PYE (JA) (OXFORD) LTD V UK (2007). PYE attempted to obtain such a financial reimbursement from the Government - for nearly one million pounds in legal fees and about the same again in lost property - The case - one might have rather obviously guessed - did not go well for PYE.

The highest Court in Europe ruled that almost all signatures to the European Constitution have a broadly similar approach to Adverse Possession and the wildly accepted view is that if a persons abandons property for a very extended period they deserve to lose it. The financial loss might be stark but the 12 years of neglect left little room for sympathy. No other nation under the Courts jurisdiction offered compensation to a disposed owner, the public policy aspect and limitation periods had; "no suggestion... [that they were]... incompatible with the convention." (At paragraph 63)

This case even allowed the EUROPEAN COURT to pour scorn on the UK's new LAND REGISTRATION ACT (2002) - At paragraph 47 it stated. "The Court cannot accept... the law of adverse possession... served no continuing public interest so far as registered land was concerned." At paragraph 74 it even questioned the UK LAW COMMISSION and LAND REGISTRY'S motives over the issue of registered lands new procedure under the 2002 ACT.

Thus - as it turned out the PYE saga finally achieved the complete opposite of the 'sexy poster boys' hype. The European court ruled that the Adverse Possession system was proportionate and the disposed owner was not entitled to compensation from the state. Indeed the ruling even went as far as to question the validity of the entire LAND REGISTRATION ACT (2002)

The manipulative whims of the higher classes have obviously been reflected in the 2002 ACT to the point where one could suggest that 'squatters' rights to peaceful possession are now in an unfairly balanced situation and centuries of public policy are in effect capable of being ignored. One could even argue a challenge in the UK Courts - and if required by the European Courts - by a determined and well-financed squatter would hold out a not unrealistic opportunity of kicking the LAND REGISTRATION ACT (2002) to death.

As WONNACOTT suggests – "The only sensible advice which can [now] be given to someone in adverse possession of a registered estate under the new regime is to keep very quiet about it, for any attempt to upgrade the 'shadow' estate will now almost certainly result in its destruction... Titles... subsisting behind the bare husk of moribund registered title... We have been here before." (Page 49) i.e. 'before' being the pre 1833 era as noted in the HISTORY section above.

"Registered land [has] once again became immune to the process of adverse possession... In practice, of course anyone who has been in undisturbed possession of someone else's land for more than 10 years would be a fool to advertise the fact to the proprietor..." Only garden boundary disputes of registered land remain under this Act. (WONNACOTT Page 141 - 2)

Neither of these statements by WONNACOTT conjure up the United Nations, European Union's or UK's desire to keep land in productive use.

THE LAND REGISTRATION ACT (2002)

Please note this Act only applies to Wales and England. It is not relevant in Northern Ireland or Scotland.

The effects of registered and unregistered land pre the LAND REGISTRATION ACT (2002) were of no significant difference in either, nature, process or evidence regardless of some of the down right stupid and pointless labels the legal types liked to slap on them in order to create differences, complexities and more revenue for themselves.

However after the ACT all NEW claims for Adverse Possession on 'registered property' altered drastically in procedure.

Claims for registered or unregistered property pre the activation date of the LAND REGISTRATION ACT (2002) (On or before the 25 Feb (2002) are not effected and remain under the LIMITATION ACT (1980).

The (2002) ACT came into force on 26 Feb (2002) based on the efforts of the LAW COMMISSION and HM LAND REGISTRY contained in a 'consultative' report – LAND REGISTRATION FOR THE 21ST CENTURY A CONVEYANCING REVOLUTION (2001) – God love the delusional fools!

The (2002) ACT basically placed all new claims for registered property into a new procedure.

All 'old' (pre 25 Feb 2002) claims for 'registered' or 'unregistered' property were unaffected.
All 'new' (post Feb 2002) claims for 'unregistered' property are unaffected.
but
All 'new' (post Feb 2002) claims for 'registered' property were now covered by the (2002) ACT

The (2002) ACT basically heavily loads the system against the squatter/possessor in preference to an absentee Landlord with a 'registered' title.

In the main the (2002) ACT seems to be pandering to the 'anti squatter' legal/political mob who after centuries of legal common sense delivering them repeated 'bloody noses' have decided to just wipe the slate clean and try a new law designed to suit their views.

It also flattered the Land Registries ego and its obvious lust for more political/legal authority. (They helped draw up this ACT.) Creating an extremely strong desire to be a 'registered' owner who would be heavily protected. Thereby establishing the likelihood of 100% land registration and the increased importance of the Land Registry and its office.

The (2002) ACT appears to reduce the right of the squatter to lodge the standard Adverse Possession claim to 10 years (down from 12) but this is not what actually happens.

The squatter makes the claim to the Land Registry –
the Registry then busy themselves – no doubt at great
tax payers expense - trying to locate the registered
paper owner so they can serve him/her a warning notice
of the squatters intentions. If this person cannot be
found or fails to object within 3 months the land
becomes the squatters but if they do object the
squatters case is defeated – automatically - without
further ado.

As WONNACOTT stated - "Registered land [has]
once again became immune to the process of adverse
possession..." (Page 141)

However

A paper owners' objection can be dismissed in
3 circumstances

1)   It would be unreasonable, due to the circumstances
      of the case, to let the paper owner dispossess the
      applicant and the applicant ought to be considered
      owner.
2)   The applicant is for some other reason entitled to
      the property.
3)   The land is adjacent to other property belonging to
      the applicant and they reasonably believed they
      actually owned such.

(One will note that point 1 makes very little sense and
points 2 & 3 seems to mirror the Scottish system of
'Prescription' were Adverse Possession is reduced to
disputes over 'garden borders.')

However if (or should I more honestly say when) the squatters claim is automatically rejected –

and

providing the said squatter does not have grounds for justifying his/her claim on the above three principles -

but

the squatter then –

–   Remains on the property for a further two years (After the date of the first objection described above.)
–   Without legal proceedings to remove them being 'in progress' (If legal action to remove the squatter is being processed it can extend the time required for Adverse Possession to become legal. As discussed in the TIME - WILLING CONFUSION ABOUT LIMITS Section.)
–   Or if such legal actions have been concluded against the squatter but not enforced within two years of the right to enforce them.

Then the squatter is entitled to become registered as owner – How's that for hoops to jump through?

Please bare in mind the paper owner is now fully aware of a squatters existence and has two years (and possibly longer) to remove them after they object to the '10 year' warning notification so kindly sent by the busy little bees at the Land Registry.

As one can see the paper owner is notified and given chance after chance to stall, suspend and kill any squatters claim. Indeed it would take a very determined (and odd) owner to lose in such circumstances. The absurdity of this being that he or she can, without fear, ignore the property on a continual basis by merely responding accordingly to the lovely warning letters sent by the helpful Land Registry people - throwing out hundreds of years of practical public policy favouring use of property over uselessness and replacing it with nothing of any substance or benefit. Indeed completely removing the threat of 'use or lose.'

The additional effect is that the 'civilised' squatter has now no motivation to regard a property as his/her own, to maintain or care for it or to act as a good neighbour because when he/she brings him/herself to the attention of the Land Registry they will notify the true owner who will – to all intents and purposes just 'take' any improvements to the property – a detrimental and totally unhelpful social side effect.

A squatter who now 'sits on in silence' for 10, 20, 40 years has no claim under Adverse Possession other than to present his/her person at the Land Registry and to have the owner notified – awarding them several months to protest the claim followed by two years (or more) to re-take possession.

The authors of this excrement of legislation claim it strikes a fairer balance between landowner and squatter and argued Adverse Possession was causing public outrage as it appeared squatters were acquiring title so easily – put sarcastically the Anti Adverse Possession riots that never occurred had deeply scared the nation so a remedy was obviously required! - ?

Any idiot who argues taking 12 long, uninterrupted years to obtain ownership is 'easy' is an idiot indeed.

Property owners who hadn't a clue of their ownership (A few and far between 'unlikely lot' for which you could have reasonable sympathy.) or reckless/uncaring owners (an all too common 'collection', for whom we should have no sympathy at all.) were now protected for the cost of a Land Registry registration fee.

This Act even had the bare faced cheek to then accept that the body of Case Law under the LIMITATION ACTS (to prove Adverse Possession) was to be accepted as the standard of proof for the (2002) ACT.

In short - this 2002 ACT is a sham - an empty, unhelpful shell.

One could however hope and trust that the practical, tried and tested allure of Adverse Possession will result in Judges wrestling with this idiotic new legal frame work only to be forced to retreat into more sane Case Law rulings which sees the return of a legal situation somewhat similar to those under the LIMITATION ACT (1980) which has, after all, been given the favourable nod from the European Courts.

One could also envisage the situation of the (2002) ACT being challenged in the Courts (Under the

HUMAN RIGHTS ACT (1988) by a squatter as 'unproportional' and heavily biased towards the willingly neglectful paper owner despite centuries of global public policy to prevent such.

As already noted in the HUMAN RIGHTS ACT (1988) section the European Courts seem eager to become involved in such a dispute over the 2002 ACT and Adverse Possession might be smiling even more when and if that day finally comes.

ADVERSE POSSESSION – STATUTE (ACTS) 'V' CASE LAW – CASE LAW WINS

The Statutes covering Adverse Possession are successful if being completely useless, unhelpful, contradictory and ignored by the Courts can be deemed as successful.

It is indeed stunning that such laws have managed to remain. It would also be a bold and honest statement to say that Adverse Possession law is almost totally based on 'Judge made' common law.

Put very briefly Common law - which is also called 'Judge made law' - is the law Judges 'make' without the express direction of a Parliament passed Statutes.

What is a 'Statute'?
In brief, as the procedures for the passing of legislation is beyond the remit of this book - A 'Bill' containing legal rules - is proposed by UK Government in the House of Commons (Or its Agencies.) and sometimes voted upon. Normally this Bill receives a majority of votes. Once it passes this vote a 'Bill' (proposed law) becomes a 'Statute' – also called 'Legislation' or an 'Act' - and becomes actual law.

Judges are supposed to enforce these Statutes and not interfere with the will of an elected Parliament. However in order to make the Statutes - which are passed by Government - workable in the real world Judges have developed a politically tolerated system of 'Judicial Interpretation.'

As we all know from 'flat pack' instruction manuals, words used to describe reality can be less than adequate and interpretation, maddening interpretation, is often required to get that coffee table built!

The process by which Judges 'make' law is called 'Judicial Interpretation'. This is a common, complex, very large and unbearably pompous and boring legal topic which is thankfully well beyond the requirements of Adverse Possession.

Even the latest legislation (LAND REGISTRATION ACT (2002)) passed by Government has done nothing to challenge Judge made common law, indeed Government willingly seems to accept the situation. Thus the (2002) ACT has merely adapted the procedure by which Adverse Possession claims can be made whilst keeping the age old 'Case Law' as the standards of proof.

However, no matter how illogical or frustrating it may be, one must bear in mind a Statue passed by Government or its Agencies may seem to say something but due to its practical application in the Courts this may not strictly be the case. It is Judge made (or common law) that is the dominant law in a Courtroom.

The best and indeed only way to uncover this dominant Judge made law is to study the outcome of individual cases. In doing so the methods of how Judges interpret Statues and apply legal tests for standards of evidence to fluid situations becomes evident. We shall explain such standards as we examine Case Law.

EXAMPLES OF CASE LAW DOMINATING STATUE IN ADVERSE POSSESSION

In Adverse Possession several such examples of Statue falling flat on its face and Judge made law marching over the top of it are evident. It is useful to explain this in order to highlight how you must remember that Statutes do not contain a full explanation of the law and may be amended by Case Law which Judges make and will follow.

THE REAL PROPERTY LIMITATION ACT (1833)

Historically the above ACT contained the 'Statue' provisions for Adverse Possession. As noted, it was far form ideal legislation. However it was then and is now the root of the Judge made 'Case Law' which still dominates the topic to this day.

We need not become to analytical of this ACT or its 'offspring' as our main interest is to show that if one learned the 'Statues' - chapter and verse - and turned up at Court hoping to play the game by the letter of these laws – he or she would be in for a very nasty shock - Judges over the centuries have twisted and amended what the terms and words of the ACT actually mean. It is this Judge made Case Law that one must grasp. You probably will never need to read a single word from the actual Statues.

EXAMPLE 1

To pick one example - within the 1833 LIMITATION ACT the words 'discontinuance' and 'dispossession' caused difficulties, which Judges, were left to decipher.

The words discontinuance and dispossession were eventually clarified in the case of RAINS V BUXTON (1880) (at paragraph 539)

<u>Disposition</u>

Roughly means a person goes in and 'drives others out' of possession rather then merely 'follows in' after a person who has already willingly left i.e. discontinuance.

However the Judge wisely argued that the two terms made no difference whatsoever as the end result was the same – 'possession' against the 'real owner.'

Over 100 years later in BUCKINGHAMSHIRE COUNTY COUNCIL V MORAN (1988) (At 644E-645C) the Judge still continued to enforce the above 'precedent.'

(Precedent, in legal terms, basically means automatically following the ruling of similar past cases to ensure consistency in Court rulings.).

This Judge also had very little time for semantics – the important point was that the 'squatter' is in actual

Adverse Possession for the time required regardless of how they came to be in this position.

Discontinuance

The MCDONNELL V M'KINTY (1847) (At 526) case witnessed the Judge stating "discontinuance" in Adverse Possession meant nothing more than abandonment by one person *followed* by actual possession by another. In short - time only starts to run and continues to run if there is an actual squatter in possession – not merely because the true owner discontinues using the property. A squatter must, at some point after the true owner has deserted the property, take possession and then keep such for a period of time as set by the prevailing law.

This ruling was still supported over a hundred years later in SMITH V LLOYD (1954) where it was again stated that there was no discontinuance of the 'paper owner' whatsoever unless there was possession by another.

Judges have therefore insured that in Adverse Possession terminology 'dispossession' and 'discontinuance' have become interchangeable terms to describe the same thing – actual physical possession by a squatter.

EXAMPLE 2

There has been other confusion over the 1833 LIMITATION ACTS wording. The ruling in the MAY V MARTIN (1885) indicated that time started to run on all land/property which was 'left to the elements' by its 'paper owner' form the date the owner actually left (i.e. as noted in the Discontinuance debate above).

This created confusion when such a decision (as clearly expressed in the actual Statute) was reached in MAY V MARTIN (1885). This ruling was quickly ignored by the Courts as 'poor law'. The MAY V MARTIN (1885) decision was deemed foolish as it basically meant any 'unused property' could be claimed at the drop of a hat by any 'passing squatter' who could show the land had been unused by the paper owner for the period required for him/her to claim the property as their own without them ever having set limb upon it.

For example a person could visit a town they had never been to before. Find an unused plot of land or other property. Do some research to uncover it had been disused by the paper owner for the required period (i.e. 12 years in Northern Ireland) and then claim it as their own – the claim would be successful as the owner was absent for more than 12 years. This is an obviously unjust result.

Therefore Judges have 'made law' and 'interpreted' the ACT to make it mean that Adverse Possession is totally dependant upon the period of time the 'squatter' is in possession. It is not in the least dependant upon how long the original owner has discontinued using the land/property. It simply relies completely on the time the squatter is in actual possession. The right to claim Adverse Possession does not begin on the date of 'discontinuance' by the real owner and it is a myth – if not worse - to state so regardless of the ACTS actual wording.

There is a certain 'get rich quick' type 'chancers' manual on Adverse Possession that I will refuse to name. This frequently surfaces via what seems to be a 'home based publisher' whose whole and quiet detailed knowledge of Adverse Possession seems dependant upon a strict reading of the English, Welsh and Northern Irish Statues. The manual then makes claims that land all over the UK (Including Scotland which is not even covered by the LIMITATION ACT at all.) is 'up for grabs.' On face value and upon checking out an official copy of the LIMITATION ACT this would appear to be the case but as we now know – Case Law has drastically altered the meaning of the LIMITATION ACT and regional variations may mean certain ACTS do not have UK wide coverage.

EXAMPLE 3

The REAL PROPERTY LIMITATION ACT (1833) also created an anomaly that still continues to resurface in the hands of some desperate and vile legal professional types.

It is endlessly argued that 'Adverse Possession' actually meant possession which was 'adverse' i.e. an 'ouster' (against/in opposition) to what the paper owner would have used the property for.

(We have discussed this and highlighted why one should remember the NEPEAN V DOE D KNIGHT (1837) case listed in the '**HISTORY – POST 1833**' section.

In short, using the property in a way the 'paper owner' would have used it made claims of Adverse Possession null. Meaning a worldly wise 'paper owner' only need the wherewithal to express the magic words - 'I would have done that.' to successfully defend any and all claims against him/her.

For example if a 'squatter' in Northern Ireland had been using a plot of land as, a theme park, farm, nuclear power plant, grave yard or an alien landing pad for more than 12 years and had made a claim for ownership to this land the 'paper owner' would merely have to state he would have also used the land for a theme park, farm, nuclear power plant, grave yard or an alien landing pad to successfully defend his/her rights. Again this would be an obviously unjust result.

The common sense, Case Law, approach to remove this unjust result has been largely successful - unfortunately it has not been a smooth, constant or even finalised process. I would even be so bold as to promise that the LAND REGISTARTION ACT (2002) will give certain people the chance to get out their voodoo sets and revive this rancid pathetic old zombie yet again.

The 'adverse to the paper owners' use of the property' argument continues to rear its head. This, in essence, is down to certain UK Judges who are arguably of a particular class, status and wealth and tend to regard any excuse - reasonable or otherwise - to defeat a 'squatters' claim as 'very suitable.' One should never disregard the self-held attitudes of some Judges in any UK Court. Indeed certain Judges, reality and common sense have often and very unfortunately proved exceptionally difficult to mix together.

As WONNACOTT would put it - "The person who is, as matter of observable fact, enjoying the benefits of the estate, 'has' or is 'in' possession of it, irrespective of whether he or she has any verifiable title or not... although it is often not stated in these terms, this is orthodox land law, as it has been understood by property lawyers since at least the 17th century." (Page 4) – Unfortunately 400+ years has not been enough time for some solicitors, barristers and judges to come to terms with this very simple and logical fact.

EXAMPLE 4

LIMITATION ACT (1980)

150 years after the 1833 LIMITATION ACT came the LIMITATION ACT (1980) – The section administering Adverse Possession was contained within this equally useless Government Statute at SCHEDULE 1 PARAGRAPHS 1 – 3.

In ultimate effect this did little to disturb the Judge made, common law that had built up in previous centuries. Judges ignored the LIMITATION (1980) ACT with all the speed to which they ignored the original REAL PROPERTY LIMITATION (1833) ACT.

SCHEDULE 1 PARAGRAPH 1 of THE (1980) LIMITATION ACT

This does little to improve the previous REAL PROPERTY LIMITATION (1833) ACT. It again suggests time starts to run from when the 'paper owner' abandons the land. Again the Courts refuse to accept such a clearly unsuitable path. Again the Courts consistently 'interpret' the flawed Statute to actually mean that another person must then take up possession before discontinuance/dispossession has fully taken place. It is at this date the clock starts to run in favour of the 'squatter.' Any periods of 'property abandonment' before the squatter actually takes possession are still not regarded by the Courts.

Indeed in the HOUNSLOW LONDON BOROUGH COUNCIL V MINCHINTON (1997) (At paragraph 232) the Judge reminded everyone that the semantics over discontinuance and dispossession were neither here nor there if not followed by actual Adverse Possession.

<u>Thus one must bear in mind that Statutes have to be read in conjunction with the Judge made case law that has been built up around them.</u>

BOUNDARIES – PROBLEMS WITH PAPER TITLE TO PROPERTY & MAPPED BOUNDARIES

This section is particularly relevant to the Scottish system of Adverse Possession, which relies on confusion over boundaries and disputed ownership due to these boundaries but is valid throughout the UK especially now that the LAND REGISTRATION ACT (2002) is in force in Wales and England as this ACT makes exceptions for such 'garden boundary' disputes, as is the case in Scotland under the concept of 'Prescription.'

It should be no surprise that the phrase 'possession is nine tenths of the law' comes form Adverse Possession claims. The first question often asked in Adverse Possession/property disputes is - who is the paper owner – who is (or could be) owner according to the deeds?

As noted in Scotland and under the LAND REGISTRATION ACT (2002) for registered land in Wales and England your case will probably depend upon such.

However for unregistered land in England or Wales and for registered or unregistered land in Northern Ireland -

before the limitation period has passed a person who can prove ownership to the higher standard will be deemed the owner – having actual deeds to this effect is extremely strong evidence of such a 'greater claim.'

A*fter* the limitation period has been exceeded the person with the higher proof of actual possession will be deemed the owner regardless of what the deeds may say.

As a result of this reality the LAND REGISTRY under LAND REGISTRATION RULES (1925) R 278 (Now applied under THE LAND REGISTRATION ACT (2002) SECTION 60) states, "...the filed plan or general map shall be deemed to indicate the general boundaries only." And "... the exact boundary will be left undetermined."

In ST. LEONARD'S V ASHBURNER (1870) (At paragraph 596) it was even stated that title deeds were of little evidential weight without evidence of the enjoyment of possession – "...parchment of itself comes too little."

Title deeds – believe it or not - are mostly treated with contempt by Courts. In WIBBERLEY (ALAN) BUILDING LTD V INSLEY (1999) they were described as – the 'hedge and ditch presumption' which was of little help and no more than a reference or at best general identification but in almost all cases had to be supplemented by proof of actual possession.

In NEILSON V POOLE (1969) it was stated 'modern conveyances are all too often indefinite or contradictory...'

The case of BRISTOW V CORMICAN (1878) at Lough Neagh in Northern Ireland had the Judge state that the Jury should even be explicitly informed that a paper owner waving about his/her deeds should be viewed as unimpressive unless he/she could prove actual possession.

In HUNTER V CANARY WHARF LTD (1994) (At 703F HL). This was expressed neatly as "...in England no law of ownership, but only a law of possession." Or, In OCEAN ESTATES V PINDER (1969), "... unwarrantable belief that title deeds are sacrosanct documents, whereas the truth is that neither a conveyance nor a land certificate retains its value if the landowner is so lax or indifferent as to lose physical control of his land."

However it must be noted that the LAND REGISTRATION ACT (2002) and the Scottish system of Prescription would certainly like to ignore these well established principles.

BOUNDARIES – FURTHER ISSUES – DOES PARTIAL POSSESSION EQUAL WHOLE POSSESSION?

If the boundaries/maps issue can be settled another problem may arise. When does occupying part of the property result in ownership of it all?

For example if a squatter takes possession of a large house or a large farm and merely uses parts of it ignoring others is it all to be deemed his/hers?

The answer would clearly seem to revolve around 'control' of the entire area. Thus if the squatter secures and maintains the boundaries and then chooses to do little, or indeed absolutely nothing at all, to that within – ownership and control are being expressed - "Where land has been abandoned, slight acts by a squatter may amount to a taking of possession" JOINT WORKING GROUP OF THE LAW COMMISSION AND THE LAND REGISTRY – Land registration for the 21st century (LAW COM NO 254 (1998) paragraph 10.4)

In CLARK V ELPHINSTONE (1880) it was held that in a large field that was totally 'hedged' off the act of hedging and no further acts or very minor acts on small parts of the field were enough to create possession –

"It is clearly settled that acts of possession done on parts of a tract [piece] of land which possessory title is sought may be evidence of possession of the whole... This rule is <u>not</u> applicable to a question of undefined and disputed boundary." (At 170)

"In many cases acts done upon parts of a district [piece] of land may evidence of the possession of the whole. If a large field is surrounded by hedges, acts done in one part of it would be evidence of the possession of the whole." (At 170)

Please note, in this case the claimant had failed to 'hedge off' the area and lost the claim. CLARK V ELPHINSTONE (1880) therefore makes it clear that when there is no such obvious evidence of defined boundaries this 'part equals whole' rule will not apply.

Thus it should be strongly noted that 'enclosing' the property and securing it against all others is an essential element of possessing the whole of the property even if only small parts of it are, or are not used with any frequency as the following cases illustrate.

In RED HOUSE FARMS V CATCHPOLE (1977) it was ruled that "Where land has apparently been abandoned... insignificant use of the land (such as occasionally mowing grass) will be sufficient to give the stranger possession of it."

These rulings were still being relied upon decades later by THE JOINT WORKING GROUP OF THE LAW COMMISSION & THE LAND REGISTRY LAND

REGISTRATION FOR THE 21st CENTURY (1998) PARA 10.4 which pointed out that; "Where land had been abandoned slight acts by the squatter may amount to a taking of possession."

This would seem to make obvious sense as WONNACOTT would suggest (Page 8) as an owner – "He/she might choose to enjoy the estate by leaving the property locked up & unoccupied."

This was established by the rulings in R V ST PANCRAS ASSESSMENT COMMITTEE (1877) and again in LIVERPOOL CORP. V CHORLEY UNION ASSESSMENT COMMITTEE (1913) Therefore it would be rather obvious that an Adverse Possessor – acting as owner - may chose to do something similar.

i.e. In SOLLING V BROUGHTON (1893) it was deemed that mere 'entries' by the owner could be classified by the Jury to be 'effective' acts of displaying control/ownership of the property. In this case no use of the land, at all, except very rare visits by the paper owner to guard against squatters was deemed to be possession against the squatters claim. The squatters chanced their luck by claiming 20 years possession when they were in fact not present as the papers owners' visits proved thereby establishing his full possession/control of the unused area. (An Adverse Possessor could also avail of this 'mere entries' ruling – i.e. he/she could lock the world out of the possession and then just occasionally patrol it to keep out/drive off all would be invaders.)

In PURBRICK V LONDON BOROUGH HACKNEY (2003) it was also noted that "... The fact that a squatter could have done more than he did... is plainly not enough of itself to defeat a claim for adverse possession otherwise, human ingenuity being what it is, virtually any claim for adverse possession could be defeated... it is not what the squatter could have done but what he did and whether what he did is sufficient too amount to physical possession... it would require a rare case where mere failure to carry out improvements to a dilapidated property or property out of repair, meant that the squatter did not have sufficient physical possession... I also consider this aspect to be irrelevant to the issue."

This was backed by ROBERTS V SWANGROVE (2007) Where it was again noted that land or property did not have to be raised to any state of profitability, domestic or commercial use.

This ruling followed the ruling of an earlier case LAMBETH LONDON BOROUGH COUNCIL V BLACKBURN 2001 where gradual improvement to the property were deemed to be of little importance as the person was in physical control of the property he was improving at his own pace as an owner would do.

HICKS DEVELOPMENT V CHAPLIN (2007) Also took the view that no, rustic or manicured improvements made no difference – control of the area in question was the issue.

The CARROLL V MARICK (1999) case confirmed it was not a case of improvements but a case of the exclusion of all others that counted.

In JONES V WILLIAMS (1837) the Judge made it clear it was for the Jury to decided upon what facts resulted in part use of the land resulting in the ownership of it all. BRISTOWN V CORMICAN (1878) confirmed this opinion.

In HIGGS V NASSAUVIAN LTD (1975) it was clearly stated there was never any legal ruling or legal principle requiring the squatter to show that he/she used all the land.

Indeed in BISSESSR V LALL (2004) this was taken to its logical conclusion when an area of 6 acres (which was clearly 'fenced in') was left idle and all but very small areas around the actual house were used – this was still deemed possession.

POSSESSION DEFINED

The 'animus possidendi' (Intention) is *normally* not an issue as it is manifested by the squatter's actual conduct – to exert effective control over the property. **(See PROPERTY USES EXPLAINED - 1) ERECTING FENCES, WALLS OR OTHER PHYSICAL BOUNDARIES/MAINTAINING BOUNDARIES** for a more detailed discussion on 'Intention.'

There are many Judgements in which the actual paper owner taking action against a <u>trespasser</u> can be effective proof of possession. In OCEAN ESTATES LTD V PINDER (1969) (At 25) stated that slight, if any, acts of possession by the paper owner meant they were 'possessing' the property and as such were permitted to take <u>trespass</u> action against <u>trespassers</u>.

However do not be fooled by the way certain legal professionals will happily mislead you over this '<u>trespass procedure</u>' – it is wholly ineffective against '<u>Adverse Possessors.</u>' Indeed a person in possession has the right to use trespass action against any absentee paper owner who suddenly turns ups.

A squatter is not 'trespassing.' He/She is not a trespasser but is in 'effective control' of the property.

The squatter is not occasionally passing by and taking whatever advantage from the property that they can but occupying it permanently as if it were their own. The Possessors therefore has the right to take Civil Court action and sue for Trespass or Nuisance – not the paper owner. (Unless he is the Possessor.)

Possessor beware - trespassers do have rights – use excess force to remove them and they can sue for Civil Court damages or even press Criminal Court charges. You are also under an obligation to be aware of trespassers safety and not to recklessly disregard such – a preposterous law for the 'litigation happy society' – the well despised cases of criminals breaking in, hurting themselves and suing as you did not make their illegal adventures in accordance with UK/European health and safety standards.

If you take a person to a Civil Court for Trespass or Nuisance the Court might award damages as it sees fit and award restitution for any damage caused. – Higher or exemplary damages are often awarded against officials – Police, Council employees etc, as a means of teaching them a lesson – they should operate with more due diligence after all.

Often suing for Trespass or Nuisance is a good way of settling boundary disputes (or collecting evidence to such disputes) even if no damages are recovered.

Thus if you are not a trespasser but a person in continual possession the real owner must stop time running by taking actual possession or by commencing the required action to recover the property. In the mean time the Possessor can rightfully ask him/her to leave.

To underline the importance of actual possession of the property the Courts have ruled that the possessor can even sell or leave his/her possession to an heir.

SALE OF POSSESSION

Possession title is transmissible – it can be 'traded' or transferred like any other commodity. In ROSENBERG V COOK (1881) the sale and such a right seemed very proper and acceptable to the Courts - "The simple fact is that the vendor had a possession… so that a fair sale of that possession is perfectly good."

HAWDON V KHAN (1920) supported this ruling, stating – "By mere virtue of possession he has title to the land… a title of which he can make a valid conveyance, and which will pass like any other property under his will or upon his intestacy."

INHERITANCE OF POSSESSION

ASHER V WHITLOCK (1865) – Leaving such a right to an heir was also deemed legitimate. This person is then entitled to possess, to defend claims made by the true owner or by any other squatter to the point where the possessor with an 'older' claim to possession can evict another 'newer' squatter who 'moves in' on the possession.

COMPULSORY PURCHASE AND THE SQUATTER

In EVANS (1873) it was ruled that a squatter in possession for over the limitation period had a right to the compensation due for compulsory purchases.

In PERRY V CLISSOLD (1907) it was judged that the possessor whose time in possession was under the limitation period had assumed the position of owner and was to be dealt with in such a manner until the true owner bettered such a position.

If the squatter is under the limitation time period the purchasing authority can agree to come to a financial arrangement i.e. in WINDER (1877) the amount was paid to the Court (Under the LAND CLAUSES CONSOLIDATION ACT (1845) SECTION 77) and held for the remainder of the 12-year limit – if the paper owner came forward it was his/hers but otherwise it became the squatters.

POSSESSION – EFFECTIVE CONTROL OF THE PROPERTY IS POSSESSION

Thus the principle is clear – the person in 'effective control' of the property – is the person who actually possess physical control over it regardless of who has the 'paper deeds.'

For example - In MOUNT CARMEL INVESTMENTS LTD V PETER THURLOW LTD (1988) (At 1084) it was ruled that the true owner instructing solicitors to write to a person in possession asking them to vacate had no effect in stopping the clock form running. "We do not accept that, in a case where one person is in possession of property, and another is not the mere sending and receipt of a letter... the recipient ceases to be in possession and the sender of the letter acquires possession."

This is blatant good sense as any person could claim possession to anyone else's property by merely sending a letter demanding such – effective control is the important matter. In this case the squatter was in control and the paper owner was merely writing silly letters.

In MARSDEN v MILLER (1992) one party took action to absorb disputed land between the two parties homes into his own property. A fence was erected - despite protests - The fence was ripped down in less than 24 hours – the dispute rumbled on and the Courts decided that 'effective control' by either party was obviously absent.

BROWNE V DAWSON (1840) had previously been the 'exhibit case' for the lack of effective control – here a school teacher had been dismissed from his position but without consent, returned to a house provided by the school. He was removed from the house by the school only to return to it. The school again removed him and he sued for trespass – the Courts ruled he had no 'effective control' and he was little more than a trespasser and the school was quite within its rights to act as it did.

In PEMBERTONE V SOUTHWARK LONDON BOROUGH COUNCIL (2000) the Council was aware the tenant was in long term arrears but this was tolerated on what amounted to simply 'kind' and 'socially responsible' grounds. (If the individual were made homeless they would have to re-home him.) The Council's reward for their acts of kindness and upkeep of the property – The tenant claimed for Adverse Possession. Fortunately the tenant's claim was deemed not sufficient to be exclusive acts of ownership against the Council and the tenant gained the result so richly deserved – a defeated claim.

In the BLIGH V MARTIN (1968) case it was made clear that 'continuous control' allowed for intervals when control was not present and in the GENERAY LTD V CONTAINERISED STORAGE COMPANY

LTD (2005) it was very wisely ruled "Adverse possession does not require... 24 hour a day physical occupation.

'SINGLE UNIT' POSSESSION IS REQUIRED TO BE EFFECTIVE

It is now an established principle that a 'single unit' must possess the property. A 'central controller' is required such as a family or some other accepted 'organised entity.'

In AG SECURITIES V VAUGHAN (1990) it was held that possession must be single, joint but not severally. Possession meant ownership by an individual, or an individual unit – family, business etc but not by a group of independent squatters who made use of the property at their own validation with no effective central control. This 'attitude' has been expressed continually by the Courts – i.e. in NORWICH CORP V BROWN (1883) (At 900) it was judged that - "To gain an adverse title under the statute of limitations the possession must not be in one man one day, and in another, another."

In LAMBETH LONDON BOROUGH COUNCIL V BIGDEN (2000). A number of squatters held keys to the property and it was judged no one person or unit was in effective possession. The Judge even commented that a 'collective' arrangement as a co-ordinated unit would be 'novel and far reaching' concept that should be rejected. (The squatters had also acknowledged the owners rights so the case failed before such an 'anti collective' ruling was required.)

The MORRIS V PINCHES CASE (1969) is deemed 'bad law' but did pour an unhelpful excretion onto the issue. Here a Judge, hell bent on defeating the squatter rather than upholding the law, argued The Pinches family was not a 'unit.' The Judge put himself in the ludicrous situation of arguing that Mr Pinch and his father and mother were a unit but the rest of the family who used the land were not. It is unlikely that such glaring stupidity will be repeated but it does, yet again, underline the mindset and intent of certain legal professionals towards Adverse Possession.

POSSESSION – EFFECTIVE CONTROL OF THE PROPERTY EVEN WHEN THE TRUE OWNER ALSO MAKES USE OF THE PROPERTY

(Also see – POSSESSION – EFFECTIVE CONTROL AND FURTHER COMPLICATIONS section.)

It is most often the case that a squatter is treated as in possession even if the owner still makes some use of the land – the issues is over effective control and a true owner making use of the land but not being in effective control does not prevent a squatter who is in effective control - despite minor breaches - being in possession. In such cases the true owner is viewed as little more than a trespasser. This is a prudent path to follow otherwise any person making any intrusion onto anyone's Adverse Possession - without consent - would continually reset the limitation period.

In HOUNSLOW LONDON BOROUGH COUNCIL V MINCHINTON (1997) the real owners' only contribution to the property was that they planted and left a 'screen hedge' to the elements. The COURT OF APPEAL ruled this was not effective control in the circumstances.

MARSHALL V TAYLOR (1895) is a very interesting case. Here the 'squatter' laid cobbles and cinders pathways, he planted flowers and used the land in a mixture of other ways. The 'paper owner' *also* made very limited use of the property to do various minor things from time to time during this entire period in question - mostly cutting the hedge. The 'squatter' won the claim for possession as he had a) enclosed the entire area and b) was in control of the area despite minor intrusions by others including the 'paper owner'.

In DOE D BAKER V COOMBES (1850). The squatter built a hut on a part of the manor however before the limitation period was up the landowner entered the hut and claimed he was now the owner of the hut. He directed that a stone should be removed from the wall and some fencing should be removed – without objection of the squatting family. The family remained in residence for another 15 years – the landowner then tried to reclaim possession. The Courts ruled that his previous acts did not constitute anything other than an entry with very minor disturbance, which did not affect the families' actual possession.

In BLIGH V MARTIN (1968) the defendant was the real owner but he did not know such. The plaintiff farmed the estate and disputed plot via local contractors – the defendant being one of these contractors - The defendant also used the land, without consent, to graze his own cattle. Upon discovering his title to ownership he argued his 'illegal' use of grazing the cattle meant he was in Adverse Possession – the Courts had no sympathy and deemed this a minor act and that he was little more than the agent of the person who had effective control of the area.

In PARADISE BEACH AND TRANSPORTATION CO LTD V PRICE – ROBINSON (1968) the PRIVY COUNCIL ruled that occasional visits and receipt of gifts from the occupiers was not enough 'effective control' to prevent squatters claiming ownership.

In TRELOAR V NUTE (1977) it was held that a squatter erecting a fence, which the owner tore down only for the squatter to rebuild and retain it did not constitute ownership or effective control by the paper owner. Also see the similar cases of ROBERTSON V BUTLER (1915) and WALKER V RUSSELL (1966) (At 527 – 28) which further underline this principle.

However

Control can be retaken by the true owner with 'effective entry' onto the property.

Were a squatter and paper owner share the land the squatter does not show the 'exclusive control' required to support his Adverse Possession claim the squatter will not succeed. This seems obvious and was underlined in the JONES V CHAPMAN (1847) (At 821)

In RANDALL V STEVENS (1853). The paper owner threw out a squatter his family and all their belongings – thus stopping time running against himself and for the squatter. The Squatter returned and remained for 13 years. This possession added to the squatters previous possession took the squatter to over the 20 year limit which was then required. The owner found out and also returned, threw the squatter out again and then went to the lengths of demolishing the cottage – possession was presumed in the owners favour as this was obviously a clear intent to actually remove the squatter and his first act of removing him had reset the clock in the land owners favour.

In WORSSAM V VANDENBRANDE (1868) a squatter erected a fence, which the owner took down. The land sat idle until the squatter returned some years later to build upon it. It was ruled that once the owner had removed the fence he had retaken possession and nothing after that act until the erection of structures by the squatter indicated otherwise.

In ALLEN V ENGLAND (1862) trees were planted and an area fenced off. It appears this was by mutual consent and the paper owner often visited and gave instruction on what was to be done in the area. It was deemed that the squatter was little more than an appointed 'bailiff' to the true owner (a fine line between this and the DOE D BAKER V COOMBES (1850) Judgement described above.)

In SOLLING V BROUGHTON (1893) it was deemed such 'entries' by the owner (Replace owner with Adverse Possessor if such is in possession) must be classed by the Jury to be 'effective' acts of displaying control of the property. In this case no use of the land except very rare visits by the paper owner to guard against squatters was deemed to be possession against the squatters claim. The squatters chanced their luck by claiming 20 years possession when they were in fact not present as the papers owners visits proved as well as establishing his full possession.

<u>Thus on a case to case basis 'effective control' of an area (Possession) is what the Courts will try to establish.</u>

POSSESSION – EFFECTIVE CONTROL & FURTHER COMPLICATIONS

We all enter almost all properties with no intention to take effective control of them.

Thus several issues can further cloud the concept of effective control. These all fall under the notion that actual entry was not a display of any intent to effectively control a property but for some other specific reason.

'Implied consent' is a term used to described the 'right' to permit people like visitors, delivery persons etc to 'encroach' your property legally as they have appropriate reason to do so. The owner can remove this implied right by asking the person to leave – if they do not leave they have then become a trespasser.

'LIMITED RIGHT' - DOES NOT EQUAL POSSESSION

In WILLIAMS V USHERWOOD (1983) a fence separated two drives. The fence was two feet (about 55cm) to far to one side (by accident) the Courts ruled this 'accident' did not matter and slight infringements by the neighbour to maintain a drain, clean windows and eaves were not sufficient to create disputed ownership

but a 'right' enforceable by ACCESS TO
NEIGHBOURING LAND ACT (1992). (Also see the
concept of applied consent in 'Statutory Powers'
chapter below.)

Likewise in MARSHALL V TAYLOR (1895) the
defendant owned adjoining land separated by a ditch.
A drain was put in the ditch and the ditch covered over
with a hedge replacing it as a boundary marker. The
hedge closed off the former part of the ditch into one
party's garden. It was deemed that cutting the hedge
and twice opening the former ditch to fix the drain
were a 'need to clean' and not actions of ownership.

**'APPLICATION OF STATUTORY POWERS' –
DOES NOT EQUAL POSSESSION**

In ADVOCATE V BLANTYRE (1879) the HOUSE OF
LORDS ruled that acts on the foreshore were 'legally
required statutory demands' and not acts of possession
against the squatter who was in full time possession.

(In short the acts wouldn't' have been done but for the
law demanding such.)

In NORTON V LONDON AND NORTH WESTERN
RLY CO (1879) the railway company entered the
squatter's possession via a hedge several times a year to
cut the grass and the hedge but did not prevent the
squatter being in possession. It was deemed that the
railway company (paper owner) had a statutory
obligation to keep such areas near the track in proper
order. They were merely doing this and not expressing

acts of ownership. '...easement required for the purpose of maintaining the hedges.'

In NESBITT V MABLETHORPE URBAN DISTRICT COUNCIL (1917). The Commissioners for sewers had to enter a property consisting of sand hills and repair sewers. They erected tool sheds and other structures. They also refused to allow building over the sewers unless by their consent. The squatter claimed the sand hills and won as the Commissioners seemed to merely be concerned with the upkeep of the sewers and performance of their statutory duties upon them and had no intention of 'owning' the sand hills.

In COLCHESTER BOROUGH COUNCIL V SMITH (1991) an opposite decision was reached but this is now deemed 'bad law'. Here the Council under the PUBLIC HEALTH ACT 1936 SECTION 15 entered property and built sewers which were then enclosed and fenced off (via contractors) The squatter was treated as having given up possession but this was not the case - the Council was not acting as land owner but under obligation of public health legislation and the ruling in NESBITT above should have been followed.

POSSESSION - EFFECTIVE CONTROL - EMPLOYEES & THOSE DEEMED AGENTS

Where a person is deemed to be an employee, tenant or agent etc and is in actual possession of a property the possession is not deemed as adverse to the true owners.

Even when the person is falsely claiming to be such an agent he/she then forfeits the claim by conceding a better claim to the actual possessor/owner. (They might also be committing fraud.)

AGENTS

In LYELL V KENNEDY (1889) a person was managing properties for 'D' but 'D' died. 'K' (Kennedy) carried on collecting rent etc and claimed to be working for 'D's' heir whoever that would eventually be. The Court ruled he had in fact formed a trust on 'D's' heirs' behalf (Lyell) and had not obtained Adverse Possession or a right to the rent collected.

In THOMAS V THOMAS (1855) an adult taking possession of land on behalf of a minor (a child) was regarded as a person acting as an 'agent' and therefore not in Adverse Possession at all.

In WARD V CARTAR (1865) a solicitor paid off a mortgage on his client's estate to facilitate a quick sale - this sale fell through. The estate was let and rent collected – the solicitor was deemed to be an agent and not in Adverse Possession.

In TINKER V RODWELL (1893) a minor (now an adult for some 36 years) was still covered by this 'trust' relationship (The relationship had not altered from the age the child had obtained adulthood.) and no Adverse Possession claim would be considered.

In short if it can be established that a person is an employee acting as an agent or acting under a 'special relationship', they cannot lodge an Adverse Possession claim that will succeed.

However

In SMITH V BENNETT (1874) it has been deemed that if the 'employee/agency' type relationship could clearly be proven as terminated the approach noted above would not be adopted.

For example, in MAGUIRE AND M'CLELLAND'S CONTRACT (1907) it was held that after a child became an adult and left the disputed property the acting agents time did start to run against the paper owner - however the possessor had to show clear and unequivocal changes in the relationship. i.e. In TINKER V RODWELL (1893), described above, the facts of the possession did not change as the person did not leave but remained within the 'trust.'

TENANTS ARE AGENTS

The situation with tenants is the same as being an agent or employee in this regard. The tenant has exclusive possession and right to exclude the Landlord but the Landlord his willingly agreed to this exchange – for the payment of rent - and retains ownership and ultimate control of the property - the tenant is merely holding it on trust/as an agent.

Indeed this concept has even been extended to the point that a Landlord can claim Adverse Possession to land near or adjoining the rented property if the tenant has taken up such possession due to the tenancy. This property is regarded as held on trust for the Landlord and must be handed over to him/her when the tenancy ends. Many cases such as SMITH V STOCKS (1869), SEDDON V SMITH (1877), HAIGH V WEST (1893), NICHOLAS V ANDREW (1920), HOLLINSHEAD V WHEAWALL (1956) have underlined this procedure.

TRUSTS

A lot of hot air could be expelled but with the same result i.e. pointing out that trustees should be treated as 'agents' and no special case should be made on this matter - Agents are described above

MORTGAGES

Put simply a person who legally has possession of a property under a mortgage but then defaults (doesn't pay) is then in Adverse Possession against the mortgage provider. The chances of a 21st century bank, building society or other such organisation 'missing' such a detail is so unlikely it is not worthy of serious consideration or discussion.

It is for this and other reasons that one could easily argue that 'mortgage cases' are no longer going to occur as a topic in the law of Adverse Possession. Indeed modern banking procedures and the legal position in the UK almost insure Adverse Possession against a mortgagee (Bank, Building Society etc) are not going to be that much of a feature on the landscape.

However

Cases were Adverse Possession is being claimed by a squatter against an owner who has a mortgage on the property offers an alternative outcome.

Where a 'paper owner' mortgages a property to a bank etc but a squatter is in possession the squatter is not party to the mortgage or to making payments under it and as such has a valid Adverse Possession claim against the paper owner and the mortgage provider.

ADVERSE POSSESSION PRE MORTGAGE

In THORNTON V FRANCE (1897) the true owner mortgaged a property, which was *already* being squatted. The Courts supported the squatter's rights over that of those who were party to the mortgage. "… The ACT does not confer a new right of entry on the mortgagee… a man in possession holding adversely to the mortgagor… has already began to run in his favour against the mortgagor."

ADVERSE POSSESSION POST MORTGAGE

In LUDBROOK V LUDBROOK (1901) and CARROLL V MANEK & BANK OF INDIA (1999) the squatter - *after* the mortgage was made - moved into possession, the possession was held to be good. However, for some totally twisted reason, the rights of the mortgage provider were then 'protected' and the squatter was deemed little more than the banks 'agent' who had merely earned the right to 'redeem' the mortgage by making full payment - including the interest. If the squatter did not do so the bank etc was entitled to possession.

In short the reoccurring unholy alliance of Politicians, Courts and Banks have decided to contort the law to protect said banks by providing sweet little exclusions for themselves – it is normally a 'holy' legal principle in

UK law that a person not party to a contract (i.e. a mortgage) cannot possibly be held liable for such - an extremely obvious and sensible view.

This ruling possibly meant that any property with a loan secured upon it is not - at all - subject to an Adverse Possession claim in the traditional sense.

However

Adverse Possession is a very practical fellow and the glaring stupidity of the above has been corrected.

In ASHE (TRUSTEE IN BANKRUPTCY OF DJABAR BADAI) V NATIONAL WESTMINSTER BANK PLC (2008) the Court decided that the above case had no logic or legal basis and may no longer be good law. In this case the squatter won his claim against the bank - "Where a mortgagor was in exclusive possession of his mortgaged property, and the mortgagee had for more than 12 years failed to protect its security by taking steps to enforce its right to possession or to obtain payment from the mortgagor, such possession was 'adverse possession' for the purposes of the Limitation Act 1980 and ran in the mortgagor's favour and against the mortgagee; and the latter's right of action, having accrued more than 12 years before, was extinguished under the Act."

ASHE was 'the person with the mortgage' for the property in question. He had 'failed' to pay the mortgage and continued to 'fail' for 12 more years meaning he could claim Adverse Possession – his claim was accepted by the Court as the 'bank' made no efforts to protect its interests.

Logically, it would therefore follow, that a 'squatter' - with no contract with the 'lending institution' - would be in an even more advantageous position than ASHE.

Thus a claim for possession in such circumstances may depend on the Judges acceptance of either the LUDBROOK or ASHE ruling. The matter has not been concluded. However it would be extremely obvious to state ASHE is the more clear cut and only logical path to follow.

POSSESSION – THE REQUIREMENT FOR CONTINUAL POSSESSION

Here the principle is very, very clear. A squatter must be in <u>continual</u> possession for the entire period required before a claim for Adverse Possession will be entertained.

In AGENCY CO LTD (TRUSTEES AND EXECUTORS) V SHORT (1888) the PRIVY COUNCIL ruled that possession must be 'continual'. If, as in this case, the 'squatter' took but then abandoned possession the effect would be as if he/she had never taken possession at all. Re-taking possession would merely 'reset' the clock to zero with no reference to past events or actions being applicable.

In short if you took possession on one date but moved out a few months later to return after several years the day of your return would be the date the Courts would deem as your only valid 'start date' for any Adverse Possession claim. If the limitation period were 12 years it would re-start on the date you returned.

Wisely this Judgement prevented a casual passing squatter chancing his/her luck by carrying out some acts in the past and vanishing only to then return later to claim they where there all along. The JOHNSON & SONS LTD V BROCK (1907) (At 538) case, the KYNOCH LTD V ROWLANDS (1912) (At 537) case and the HOUNSLOW LONDON BOROUGH COUNCIL V MINCHINTON (1997) (At 232) etc, etc have all insured the 'continual possession' rule is set in stone.

Dissenting views to this, such as that expressed in LEIGH v JACK (1879) (At 272) have not been tolerated, deemed very 'poor law' and are now totally dismissed. The Judge in this case, unusually, attempted to support the squatter's stance and argued slight acts followed by abandonment were sufficient for an Adverse Possession claim – his view was not well received at all.

In short you must 'continually' occupy the property for the limitation period required – without exceptions.

However as already pointed out in the BLIGH V MARTIN (1968) case it was made clear that 'continuous control' allowed for intervals when control was not present and in the GENERAY LTD V CONTAINERISED STORAGE COMPANY LTD (2005) it was very wisely ruled "Adverse possession does not require... 24 hour a day physical occupation."

Evidence for what constitutes 'continual possession' are provided in the **'EVIDENTIAL MATTERS IN ADVERSE POSSESSION CASES'** section below.

POSSESSION – WHAT IS ADVERSE?

Again Case Law (as opposed to actual Statues) proves the dominant force. The various ACTS i.e. The REAL PROPERTY LIMITATION ACT (1833) or the LIMITATIONS ACT (1980) SCHEDULE 1 PARAGRAPH 8 have been defined to mean that time only runs against the 'paper owner' if the land is in 'continuous' Adverse Possession. The term 'continuous' was quickly defined (See above.) - However the word 'adverse' has also proved to be very open to interpretation.

As noted in the chapter explaining THE REAL PROPERTY LIMITATION ACT (1833) – handing people - like certain Judges or other legal professionals - any discretion at all is an extremely disappointing and costly (or in their case profitable) experience. They will make a meal (or mess) of all such possible occasions.

The single word 'adverse' in Adverse Possession is such an example of these 'geniuses at work.' They have had several hundred years (and counting) of debate and analysis – definition has been clearly established - but still they have not accepted this definition. They know full well what the term means in an established, practical and workable way but frequently just chose not to use it and continually make efforts to argue black is white.

What is 'adverse' in reference to possession?

We will take the path that Courts normally end up 'forced' to take, when common sense grips, before explaining certain smug practices, which ultimately fail but continue to resurface.

To most it would be a very simple explanation - a squatter using the property as if it were their own and without explicit consent of the 'real owner' is in 'continual' 'adverse' 'possession' to the paper owner who is not exercising possession and control of the said property or land. (Or in Scotland where one of at least two possible 'paper owners' has lost control to the other.)

Possession and Adverse is?

A person who is in actual 'possession' of the property may be there completely legally i.e. renting a hotel room, renting a house, leasing a field, living with parents, living with relatives or friends - with consent – these are all forms of 'legal possession' which cannot be adverse as the owner has at some level consented.

In COREA V APPUHAMY (1912) the PRIVY COUNCIL clearly stated that the decision in THOMAS V THOMAS (1855) held true – possession, if lawful is not adverse and cannot be allowed to be so - or any person, entering lawfully and remaining lawfully could claim Adverse Possession.

For example you could buy a house with a mortgage or rent it and after 12 years claim it was your own - refusing to pay additional rent or mortgage payments – an obviously very unsuitable legal situation.

The Courts have been keen to expand the THOMAS V THOMAS (1855) (At 83) principle to other cases where it is questionable if the squatter was in possession lawfully or not i.e. the burden of proof is forced upon the squatter to prove it was illegal/ wrongful.

In the MAGDALEN HOSPITAL (PRESIDENT & GOVERNS) V KNOTTS (1878) it was ruled that in 'questionable cases' of this nature it was for the squatter to present proof of such. In this case the 'real owner' had granted leases for 149 years on 'peppercorn rent.' The squatter claimed he had not entered under this lease and knew nothing of it, it was deemed he had to prove this rather than merely assert it or the Courts would be back in the situation as described in the MAY V MARTIN (1885) case – were a squatter could claim possession on any unused property almost at will by merely stating he was in possession for the required period and needed no evidence to prove such.

For example in PYE (JA) (OXFORD) LTD V GRAHAM (2000) it was argued that if a person was 'legally' allowed to graze cows but then grazed sheep that no action would arise as the so called Adverse

Possession was not of any real substance merely a breach of the agreement/lease.

However if a neighbour allowed a person onto his land for certain purposes over a certain period of time i.e. grazing animals for one year and the person remained for another 12 + years, without agreement or making payment etc, that would be heavy evidence of illegality and Adverse Possession.

So 'Adverse Possession' is?

Adverse Possession therefore must represent some level of 'illegality' i.e. the 'squatter' should not legally be there.

(This is not the case in Scotland where some element of 'title/legality' is required before Adverse Possession can be considered.)

This person, if they can prove such illegality, can then rely on the clock running in his/her favour against the true 'paper owner.' Thus time can run in favour of a person in possession of property due to two very broad scenarios -

1) Where a 'squatter' never had the legal right to be in possession but has taken up such i.e. a 'squatter' deliberately or by error moves into and secures a house or flat etc as his residence. Or fences off and farms a plot of land etc, etc.

2) Where the person was originally in legal possession but the possession becomes unlawful i.e. a person

who moved in as a legal rent paying tenant then fails to pay the rent but remains in the property.

These two brief descriptions hide a multitude of weird and wonderful circumstances but are very accurate depictions of how Adverse Possession arises - Either you simply take possession illegally or whilst in legal possession you end up in illegal possession.

The essential element here is that the possession is or becomes 'wrongful.' RAMNARACE V LUTCHMAN (2001) the Judge stated; "...generally speaking, Adverse Possession is possession which is inconsistent with and in denial of the title of the true owner. Thus possession is not adverse if it is enjoyed by a lawful title or with the consent of the true owner."

In BUCKINGHAMSHIRE COUNTY COUNCIL V MORAN (1988) it was reduced to a very neat description - 'Possession in the wrong.'

However

There are exceptions that depend upon individual cases.

Chiefly these amount to 'tolerated trespass.' This term was established by the HOUSE OF LORDS in BURROWS V BRENT LONDON BOROUGH COUNCIL (1996) – it was used to define a person in possession - that could have been - but was not Adverse Possession due to the facts of the case. The 'squatter' kept arranging to pay arrears but failed to do so, however by admitting he owed arrears to the real owner he conceded he was not in Adverse Possession.

In PEMBERTONE V SOUTHWARK LONDON BOROUGH COUNCIL (2000) the Council was aware the tenant was in long term arrears but this was tolerated on what amounted to simply 'kind' and 'socially responsible' grounds. (If the individual were made homeless they would have to re-home him.) The Council's reward for their acts of kindness and upkeep of the property – The tenant claimed for Adverse Possession. Fortunately the tenant's claim was deemed not sufficient to be exclusive acts of ownership against the Council.

Unnecessary problems

The above examples may appear clear and logical. But clear and logical is not the 'pay day' legal professionals or 'power of discretion' Judges happily wield over the general 'peasantry.'

Adverse can, idiotically, be defined in another way. (As we have touched upon before – see '**THE REAL PROPERTY LIMITATION ACT (1833) in the 'HISTORY'** section.) It can be argued that Adverse Possession means adverse to the 'paper owners' 'use' of the property. A 'smart ass' play on words which, is ultimately hollow, snide and arrogant - but very profitable.

For example if an individual possess a farm for 50 years. Worked and maintained it and neither sees nor hears from the 'paper owner' and then makes a claim to become the properties true registered owner the 'paper owner' would merely have to state that it was a farm, he/she would have used it as such and the claim would fail as farming was not adverse to the 'papers owners' use of the land. This is an obviously disgusting 'get out of jail free' card for any absentee paper owner.

Judges and legal professionals have been continual in their efforts to argue such an absurdity and not without successes. As already noted previously a worldly wise 'paper owner' could swear blind his/her 'intent' for the property had always matched the 'squatters actions' regardless of what the squatter actions were and who could prove the paper owner and his/her intents were untrue?

In PYE (JA) (OXFORD) LTD V G GRAHAM (2000) the Judge (yet again) stated that possession needn't live up to this contemptible definition of 'adverse' and the desires of the paper owner were meaningless. That 'ousting' (removing) the owner merely meant acting as the true owner yourself and doing as you pleased with your property – the essence of ownership. The Judge refused to entertain the argument that committing deeds 'adverse' to what the true owner might have done were required and argued it was little more than a can of worms that needn't be opened.

In TRELOAR V NUTE (1977) it was also ruled ridiculous to argue possession depended on having to 'annoy' the real owner in some manner. No authority has ever been established to cite such. This would simply allow the paper owner to say he/she was not annoyed to win any such claim against them. "Indeed if inconvenience to the owner had to be established it would be difficult ever to acquire a … title since the owner if inconvenienced would be likely to take proceedings." (Perversely and deliberately this 'annoyance' is exactly the opportunity the LAND REGISTRATION ACT (2002) now provides for registered property owners in England and Wales.)

The view taken in the TRELOAR V NUTE (1977) case was that the squatter is in possession and entitled to act as they seen fit upon the property. This is a logical view as requiring them to act contrary to whatever the 'paper owners' desires would be -

a) Impossible as the paper owner could just state 'I was going to do that.'
b) Requires the squatter to deliberately act in some very unusual and impractical ways in order to protect their claim. This surely defeats the essence of 'ownership' when you are 'forced' to do things beyond what you would normally do if you had owned the property.
c) It also opens a catch 22 situation were it could be argued a squatter acted perversely as they knew they were not the real owner and have thereby conceded - by an implied acknowledgement - a better claim to the property.

It would also be very, very foolish to claim the term 'adverse' has finally been nailed down by the PYE (JA) (OXFORD) LTD V G GRAHAM (2000) case, the preceding European rulings and the hundreds of years of history that preceded this judgement. The term has been killed repeatedly over the past few hundred years but still continues to make itself appear.

POSSESSION – SUCCESSIVE SQUATTERS

THE LIMITATIONS ACT (1980) SCHEDULE 1 PARAGRAPH 38 (5) States if 'Individual A' takes Adverse Possession and deserts it and then Individual B takes up possession B cannot add his time in possession to A's.

In FAIRWEATHER V ST MARYLEBONE (1962) it was stated that the new possessor – individual B - could not add his possession to individual A's. This ruling was underlined in MULCAHY V CURRAMORE PTY LTD (1974).

This follows the logic that possession must be continuous.

However

As discussed earlier if 'Individual A' gives, sells, leaves in a will or transfers etc, etc his right to 'Individual B' – continuous possession is not broken and continues. Indeed no 'formal' agreement over such an exchange was required. In AGENCY CO LTD (TRUSTEES & EXECUTORS) V SHORT (1888) it was argued that the Adverse Possessors had to prove title was in continuance and derived automatically from one to the other i.e. sold to or inherited by the next possessor.

EVIDENTIAL MATTERS IN ADVERSE POSSESSION CASES

Great variation and infinite hair splitting could be contributed to subject headings for what uses of a property constitutes evidence of actual possession. This would be a futile exercise considering the desired result – to establish the pros and cons of various circumstances in relation to actual possession.

Fortunately Adverse Possession Case Law - based on Court practice - provides us with legal situations that insist upon reoccurring and therefore warrant closer inspection. It is worth noting variations upon these themes and the entrance of new examples offer virtually limitless possibilities and problems.

It is important to point out that these are generalised, self appointed, topic headings and form no infinite index but act as a framework for how a 'new' case might be handled.

This analysis may create the illusion of completely contradictory decisions and cause initial confusion but when cases are individually dissected it becomes evident that 'clear black and white' decisions are more common than 'murky grey ones' so be patient as you work your way through the topics.

The law – more often than not – is extremely over complicated. A glib, brief overview of actual cases - normally well scattered throughout the book in question is distressingly inconclusive and completely frustrating to the 'human' reader. (That is why 'legal beings' tend to write books in such a manner.) Therefore each of the authors shamelessly 'self appointed' topics have been laid out in a standardised pattern, put in systematic order - all in the one place for your referencing ease and speed.

Thus –

1) The weight of evidence for possession is clearly stated first.
2) Cases that obtain this standard are then cited and briefly discussed.
3) Finally cases that failed to meet the grade are discussed. This pass/fail 'working model' of Adverse Possession cases is akin to the decisions applied by the Courts
4) It will become obvious that in reality Adverse Possession law provides very limited 'grey areas.' Where such areas are evident the readers' attention is drawn to such and the murky anomaly explained.

It is also essential that you grasp the fact that each individual case will turn upon its own circumstances. There are no solid standards in fluid situations.

BURDEN OF PROOF

It is upon the squatter to bring and prove their claim. Once this has been done it is for the defence to try and prove better title.

Were a squatter has clear evidence to possession which stretches beyond the limitation period he/she can apply to have the oppositions claim struck out – RICHES V DPP (1973) or to request a declaration Judgement that the true owners title is extinguished and he/she is entitled to remain in possession as under PART 24. CIVIL PROCEDURES RULES (1998)

USES OF PROPERTY WHICH
CONSTITUTE POSSESSION

This Section is relevant throughout the UK and forms the basic building blocks of a case for or against Adverse Possession/Prescription.

After reading this section you should, hopefully, be very capable of picking out the 'facts' of a case and accessing their evidential worth depending on the individual circumstances of any new situation presented to you.

For no particular reason the Case Law has been placed into different generalised topics in the hope they will lead to a quicker referencing of evidence that may cross your path.

1) Erecting fences, walls or other physical boundaries/ Maintaining boundaries
2) Locking gates, doors and controlling access
3) Building, seeking planning permissions, paving etc
4) Cultivation of land for crops/garden
5) Planting trees
6) Parking
7) Paying tax/council rates/utilities bills/ground rents etc
8) Storage

9) Erecting notices
10) Cutting trees, turf or grass
11) Grazing
12) Play & Recreation areas/Fishing/Shooting
13) Granting leases etc, employees, agents and other special relationships
14) Local costume/Historical factors
15) Electoral Register

From the outset it is worth underlining that the first 5 of these topics are often, but not always, defined as 'hard' evidence for possession claims. The first 2 are particularly important.

Without one, or more, of these 'big 5' running in your favour for the continual time frame required before an Adverse Possession claim can be made any 'hopeful squatters' case may well be on very dubious grounds.

The other topics are often, but not always deemed as 'supportive' evidence.

PROPERTY USES EXPLAINED

1) ERECTING FENCES, WALLS OR OTHER PHYSICAL BOUNDARIES/MAINTAINING BOUNDARIES

'Cutting of' an area of property and securing it from the world at large is basically the core essence of actual possession and as such *extremely* strong evidence.

The construction of fences, walls or other such physical boundaries, i.e. ditches, dikes, hedges etc, etc and maintaining such are deemed as probably the most 'concrete' type of evidence of openly possessing a property to the exclusion of all others.

'Adopting' and maintaining existing walls, fences or hedges etc, etc is also deemed as a strong desire to possess with exclusion of all others.

Erecting Fences is usually an unequivocal act of possession as stated in POWELL V MCFARLANE (1997) (At 477 – 78.) Where the Judge stated that this act was so drastic, that unless there was contrary evidence it unquestionably pointed to 'appropriation for the erector' of such a physical boundary. This is certainly the historically and contemporary 'standard' view which is applied again and again by Judges.

If you are serious about your Adverse Possession – this is your biggest and most dangerous weapon - lock the world out and wait for the limitation period to elapse.

In WILLIAMS V USHERWOOD (1983). A fence, which was replaced by a wall, was erected between two houses. However it was mistakenly built in the wrong place. The Judge stated the construction of such was; "strong evidence" even if the erection area was; "… founded on a mistaken premise does not help the paper owner." In short a fence or wall etc built in the wrong place by *accident*, still gives rise to a claim of Adverse Possession and is strong evidence for its success.

In WALLIS'S CAYTON BAY HOLIDAY CAMP LTD V SHELL-MEX AND BP LTD (1975). It was argued that cleaning ditches, cutting hedges and grass, collecting rubbish. Repairing and painting fences amounted to factual possession as it was a significant assertion of control.

In LEE V PARSONS (1998). A ditch was cleaned, widened, altered and access to it refused to others, including the actual paper owner, so it was agreed that the claimant was its owner.

Filling in a ditch was also seen as a clear act of ownership in CUNLIFFE V LONDON AND NORTH WESTERN RLY CO. (1888)

PRUDENTIAL ASSURANCE CO LTD V WATERLOO REAL ESTATE INC (1999). A dispute over a wall was settled in Waterloo's favour due to a list of works carried out upon it - 1) The wall to any objective observer appeared to be incorporated into their premises - 2) Works to the wall went beyond minimal – Increased height, attached gutter, attached roof, removing graffiti and general cleaning/maintenance - 3) Attaching a security camera, lighting and entry-phone system - 4) Cutting through wall to insert a night safe and overflow pipe were all acts of ownership.

However

As each case turns on it own quirks, the issue is slightly more complex than it first appears.

Fencing etc is not always 'strong' evidence due to the individual circumstances of the case. The heavily sited case in this area is BASILDON DISTRICT COUNCIL V CHARGE (1996) where it was argued a 'goose fence' was to weak and temporary to constitute a serious attempt of exclusion. Basically a length of string suspended between pegs, which are pushed, at intervals, into the ground was not deemed a 'real' or suitably substantial fence.

Maintaining a boundary – fence, wall, hedge, ditch etc is not always deemed an act of exclusion. In BOOSEY V DAVIS (1987). Patching a fence and putting additions to it were deemed 'weak' evidence of possession especially when it did not enclose the entire area in question. The conduct must go beyond mere 'basic/bare minimum' maintenance or repair and reach the point of exclusive possession

In short fence the 'entire area' in 'properly' or you will probably lose your case - There is very little point having a big gun and no ammunition!

Similar cases have also been regarded as falling short of exclusive possession. In SEARBY V TOTTENHAM RLY CO (1868) and LITTLEDALE V LIVERPOOL COLLEGE (1900) the trimming or clipping of hedges – in these cases - was not significant enough a deed on its own for a claim of Adverse Possession.

In CRAVEN V PRIDMORE (1902) patching up fences with occasional rough repairs was, in this case, deemed as shadowy and neutral attempts towards real physical possession.

In BLADDER V PHILIPS (1991) it was argued that a quick and occasional cleaning of a ditch, in this case, was not sufficient to amount to possession.

WILLIAMS BROS DIRECT SUPPLY LTD V RAFTERY (1958) – a line of bricks were set out to mark the boundary – deemed 'minor.'

Exceptions to 'securing boundaries'

In SEDDON V SMITH (1877) the Judge stated, that 'enclosures', i.e. fencing, walls etc did not always matter. He agreed it was the; "... strongest possible evidence." But noted this particular case was based on land which was ploughed and planted but never enclosed. The individual facts of this particular case proved that this was the 'standard' historical costume/ practice for this type of land in that region and therefore possession with intent was clearly displayed within an area that could be clearly defined despite lack of formal fencing etc.

Problems with the above situation.

As if each case turning on its own facts is not complicated enough other problems have surfaced in relation to 'boundaries' as regards motivation/intent of the 'squatter' involved. In the main these show the desire of Judges to defeat the squatter 'come what may' rather than any application of common logic or spirit of the law.

As JOURDAN would point out via his colleague RADLEY-GARDNER despite its lengthy legal history 'intention' has never been securely defined in any concrete way. JOURDAN wisely states that in Adverse Possession cases MINCHINTON (LONDON BOROUGH OF HOUNSLOW V MINCHINTON (1997)) is the only logical path to be followed and thus the much preferred ruling i.e. if the possessor had secured the area by mistake or design for the required time their intent was to be taken for granted and was not to be disputed.

Some Judges have been less sensible or certain in their outlooks.

In WIMPEY (GEORGE) & CO LTD V SOHN (1976) the Court of Appeal argued the intention of the claimant could play a part due to the circumstances of the case. The claimant has to take actual possession of the area but if they were motivated to merely fix a hole in an existing fence the intention too fence of an area and to exclude all others/possess it was not met regardless of what their actions achieved. (The SOHN case is an unusual one as other factors did point to the fact they had never tried to claim possession over the area they had completely fenced in and had on several occasions conceded ownership to WIMPEY - thus they lost their case based on these facts.)

The FRUIN V FRUIN (1983) case is more clear cut. Once again the claimants motivation was taken into account – A fence and gate were, somehow, deemed by the Court to be no more than a 'marker' to keep animals away from the main farmhouse and open road. The Court of Appeal also agreed that the fence was never intended as an act of exclusive possession.

The ADAMS V TRUSTEES OF MICHAEL BATT CHARITABLE TRUST (2001) also followed the same reasoning with regards to a similar situation over a fence as did CRAVEN V PRIDMORE (1902) where patching up fences with rough repairs - with the intent to keep stock in was – somehow - not enough for a possession claim.

The 3 cases above appear to contradict WILLIAMS V USHERWOOD (1983). A fact not missed in the following case.

In HOUNSLOW LONDON BOROUGH COUNCIL V MINCHINTON (1997) the judge rejected FRUIN/

ADAMS style arguments - 'Their motive is irrelevant.' The important thing was the fact they were treating the land as theirs and excluding all others continually for the period required. In this particular case the defendants admitted their intent was to keep dogs in rather than others out – they still won as, rather logically, they had in effect insured exclusive use of the area – the fence that held the dogs in also held the rest of the world out.

Therefore it appears obvious that nothing is obvious and the Courts still have some way to go before 'cementing' a position. Put simply the Court may -

a) Take into consideration what they deem to be the motivation of the claimant i.e. the FRUIN V FRUIN (1983) style cases. Where it seems the Judge will 'kindly' tell you what your intent was.

b) Or it may regard such motivation/intent as utterly irrelevant to the reality of the claim - a much more logical and obvious path i.e. as already stated in the HOUNSLOW LONDON BOROUGH COUNCIL V MINCHINTON (1997) case or the 'accidentally in possession' case of WILLIAMS V USHERWOOD (1983). Both cases meant they had met the evidential quota required and the claim should succeed regardless of their intent.

This is an undesirable position and it should be argued that the FRUIN V FRUIN (1983) type cases are very 'poor law' which is unsustainable and confusing.

Any claimant with an ounce of common since could merely - and wisely - insist it was his/her full intention to 'openly possess and exclude all others' to avoid any such complications over this issue.

Equally any paper owner with no real defence could quickly argue the 'squatter' had no intention to possess - with the result of an expensive Court case to prove otherwise.

It also leaves such cases open to the complete discretion of the Judge and his/her prejudices - an entirely deplorable situation in itself.

The fact the claimant has actually put him/herself into 'exclusive and continual possession' by any means - half heartedly i.e. HOUNSLOW LONDON BOROUGH COUNCIL V MINCHINTON (1997) or accidentally i.e. WILLIAMS V USHERWOOD (1983) should mean they have meet the evidential quota required for possession.

Fortunately the MINCHINTON/USHERWOOD examples also seem to be the path the courts are now inclined to favour - "The only intention which has to be demonstrated is an intention to occupy and use the land as one's own." WRETHAM V ROSS (2005)

2) LOCKING GATES/CONTROLLING ACCESS

Holding the right of access to property is very strong evidence of possession - another 'big weapon' for the Adverse Possessor.

In POWELL V MCFARLANE (1997) the Judge ruled that locking and blocking entry was drastic evidence.

In BUCKINGHAMSHIRE COUNTY COUNCIL V MORAN (1988). Moran put a chain and padlock on a gate and sealed of the land except for access from his own garden (Or by climbing dikes, hedges and fences surrounding the plot.) The Judge ruled that; "Placing a new lock and chain on the gate… In my Judgement… did amount to a final and unequivocal demonstration of the defendant's intention to possess the land."

In BEVAN V LONDON PORTLAND CEMENT CO LTD (1892) Control of access - even if unlocked – was deemed unambiguous assertion of ownership – especially as he often turned trespassers away. Similarly in DES BARRES V SHEY (1873) vigorous steps were taken to prevent anyone else entering or remaining without consent. When a hut was built without their knowledge or consent they sued for possession (successfully) and when trees were cut without their permission they prosecuted for trespass (successfully.)

More domestically in LAMBETH LONDON BOROUGH COUNCIL V BLACKBURN (2001). A squatter 'removed' - one might say he broke in - the Councils front door lock to a domestic flat and replaced it with his own 'Yale' lock – this was deemed unequivocal proof of exclusion of all others.

However

As explained in the previous chapter (**ERECTING FENCES, WALLS OR OTHER PHYSICAL BOUNDARIES/MAINTAINING BOUNDARIES -**

Problems with the above situation.) The FRUIN V FRUIN (1983) case and other cases did take the claimants motivation into account. The FRUIN ruling and other such cases, in my humble opinion are an unwelcome anomaly and are without question 'poor law' – however one should remember that they could still be used at a Judges whim.

For example a very twisted Judge could have ruled BLACKBURN was merely motivated by the need for 'shelter' but had no intent to adversely occupy. Indeed Judges could apply this 'no actual intent' business to nearly all Adverse Possession claims and routinely dismiss them at will – Judges should not be permitted to inform you of your intent when your actions are obvious.

3) BUILDING, SEEKING PLANNING PERMISSIONS & PAVING ETC

Paving or building etc is seen as a clear act of ownership.

In THEW V WINGATE (1862), a barn was built, fences, a cottage and a pond were constructed – these were deemed as very obvious signs of possession.

In WILLIAMS V USHERWOOD (1983) 'paving' was also deemed 'good evidence' as was 'concreting' in TAYLOR V LAWRENCE (2001).

In LAING & LAING V MORAN & MORAN (1952) it was ruled that even when the building was only used occasionally with periods of none use it still amounted to good evidence for possession.

Carrying out work to prepare for actual building may also help. In TRELOAR V NUTE (1977) – land was levelled to prepare for building works – this equalled possession.

Indeed in CULLEN V CULLEN (1962) a father told his sons mother to build a house on his land at any place they pleased as the property would be left to them when he died. The house was built but then the father changed his mind and claimed possession. The Judge poured scorn on his complete violation of decency and 'estopped' him from claiming the building (Estoppel is a legal term for preventing a party from doing something under threat of legal punishment.) The Judge argued that if the mans act was to succeed he would open an unholy can of worms where consent could be given and then removed and any property built in the mean time could be 'stolen'. The Judge also pointed out after 12 years the son could apply and would be successful in an Adverse Possession case with reference to the house.

However

Merely erecting a structure doesn't always count. Each case turns on it own facts and if such construction is not extensive enough they may be dismissed.

In LITTLEDALE V LIVERPOOL COLLEGE (1900) the erection of a single telegraph pole with no other evidence of use or ownership of the land was deemed poor evidence.

The same ruling was made in SINDALL (WILLIAM) PLC V CAMBRIDGESHIRE COUNTY COUNCIL (1994) when a single pipe was laid and this constituted the entire and unconvincing claim for control and ownership for the period in question.

Other 'constructions' and the use of them may also be insufficient - for example in STACEY V GARDNER (1994) a furnace was built and used but lacked the significance required in that particular case.

The ACCESS TO NEIGHBOURING LAND ACT (1992) gives you legal rights to enter a neighbours land to carry out essential maintenance on your own property so any situation that could be considered under this ACT is unlikely to support an Adverse Possession claim.

In ADVOCATE V BLANTYRE (1879) the HOUSE OF LORDS ruled that acts on the foreshore were 'legally required statutory demands' and not acts of possession against the squatter in full time possession. (In short the acts wouldn't' have been done but for the law demanding such.)

In NORTON V LONDON AN NORTH WESTERN RLY CO (1879) the railway company entered the squatters' possession via a hedge several times a year to cut the grass and the hedge but did not prevent the squatter being in possession. It was deemed that the railway company (paper owner) had a statutory obligation to keep such areas near the track in proper order. They were doing this and not expressing act of ownership. "…easement required for the purpose of maintaining the hedges."

In NESBITT V MABLETHORPE URBAN DISTRICT COUNCIL (1917) The Commissioners for sewers had to enter property consisting of sand hills to repair sewers. They erected tool sheds and other structures in areas. They also refused to allow building over the sewers unless by their consent. The squatter claimed the sand hills and won as the Commissioners seemed to be concerned with the upkeep of the sewers and performance of their statutory duties upon them and had no intention of 'owning' the dunes.

4) CULTIVATION for CROPS/GARDEN

This involves 'breaking the surface' of the soil and planting (amongst other related things) and amounts to complete physical control of the land so is strong evidence for possession.

The Courts are consistent in ruling that gardening or farming land constitutes possession as in POWELL v MCFARLANE (1997) or SEDDON V SMITH (1877)

The SMITH V STOCKS (1869) case revolved around a disused gravel pit that had been filled with soil, this was perhaps not enough evidence alone to secure 'possession' however it was then used to grow crops in – this was deemed sufficient for possession.

NORTON V LONDON AND NORTH WESTERN RLY CO (1879). Norton used land as a garden, which he hedged off. He won his case and the Court of Appeal deemed it a 'complete case of possession.'

MARSHALL V TAYLOR (1895) is a very interesting case. Here the 'squatter' laid cobbles and cinder pathways, he planted flowers and used the land in a mixture of other ways. The 'paper owner' *also* made very limited use of the property to do various minor things from time to time during this entire period in question. The 'squatter' won the claim for possession as he had a) enclosed the entire area and b) was in control of the area despite minor intrusions by others including the 'paper owner'.

In SEDDON V SMITH (1877) the Judge stated, that 'enclosures', i.e. fencing, walls etc did not always matter. He agreed it was the; "… strongest possible evidence." but noted this particular case was based on land which was ploughed and planted but never enclosed. The individual facts of this particular case proved that this was the 'standard' historical costume/ practice for this type of land in that region and therefore possession with intent was clearly displayed within an area that could be defined despite lack of formal fencing etc.

In NEILSON V POOLE (1969) grass mowing – if it left a distinct line between two 'open' boundaries - could be seen as evidence of acts of ownership to that plot of land.

Like - **3) BUILDING, SEEKING PLANNING PERMISSIONS & PAVING ETC** - the extent of the 'cultivation' must be obvious. Fortunately noticing if an area is cultivated or not is usually very obvious.

However

In HOUNSLOW LONDON BOROUGH COUNCIL V MINCHINTON (1997) the real owners' only contribution to the property was that they planted and left a 'screen hedge' to the elements. The COURT OF APPEAL ruled this was not effective control in the circumstances.

Tree sprawl i.e. branches growing onto other land was not possession as in LEMMON V WEBB (1895). Nor was merely collecting fallen wood as in GROSE V WEST. (1816)

5) PLANTING TREES

In ST LEONARDS V ASHBURNER (1870) planting tress was deemed as equal to building a fence or wall and very strong evidence of possession.

However

In HOUNSLOW LONDON BOROUGH COUNCIL V MINCHINTON (1997) the real owners' only contribution to the property was that they planted and left a 'screen hedge' to the elements. The COURT OF APPEAL ruled this was not effective control in the circumstances.

Tree sprawl i.e. branches growing onto other land was not possession as in LEMMON V WEBB (1895). Nor was merely collecting fallen wood as in GROSE V WEST. (1816)

6) PARKING

Normally seen as unimportant.

In PAVLEDES V RYESBRIDGE PROPERTIES LTD (1989) it was deemed that P had made a 'secret' entrance to a closed of area. He then used this to park on. He also permitted others to park on a small area of the whole site. Eventually he built a proper entrance. His 'secret' rather than 'open possession' meant the Court would not accept his claim.

However

If he had been honest and open about his possession and made proper use of the area including maintaining the fences as if they were his own his case would probably have been viewed in a different light and the parking would have been supportive evidence for such.

This was the case in WILLIAMS V USHERWOOD (1983) when a fence, by mistake, was erected in the wrong place and enclosed a two-foot strip (about 55 cms) of driveway, which lay between two houses. This was used for parking and teamed with the fence was deemed to be 'exclusive control.' (Arguably the fence was the more important factor.) TAYLOR V LAWRENCE (2001) is a similar case to WILLIAMS

V USHERWOOD (1983) further underlining the
principle.

In LAING & LAING V MORAN & MORAN (1951)
a worn 'earth track' in the grass leading to a garage was
deemed strong evidence for possession for both the
garage and the land because the 'worn track' crossed
over the property to reach the garage.

7) PAYING TAX/COUNCIL RATES/UTILITY BILLS/GROUND RENTS ETC

Australia, the USA and other nations do hold such
payments as very significant but the UK is weary of
such as it is not deemed as evidence of actual psychical
residence as stated in the LOCAL GOVERNMENT
FINANCE ACT (1992) Section 6. In short you could
pay the bill but be living elsewhere. The USA etc is just
happy for the payment it would otherwise not have
received - the UK requires stronger evidence of
residence.

In KIRBY V COWDEROY (1912) (A Canadian case
which was heard by the PRIVY COUNCIL of the UK.)
It was ruled that such payments did constitute a factual
element of physical possession. In the UK - ALLAN V
LIVERPOOL OVERSEERS (1974), R V ST
PANCREAS ASSESSMENT COMMITTEE (1877) and
LAING (JOHN) & SON LTD V KINGSWOOD
ASSESSMENT COMMITTEE (1949) It was deemed
that 'rate paying' was indeed good evidence of
occupation if it could be linked to actual physical
possession but paying taxes whilst not being in
possession would not count as evidence of possession.

The leading case for such is probably WESTMINSTER CITY COUNCIL V TOMLIN (1989) where a squatter deemed to be in possession became liable for such payments under the LOCAL GOVERNMENT (FINANCE) ACT Section 6 (2) (1992). Thus his possession was directly linked to him being obliged to pay the rate bill.

STATUTES in the UK impose a duty to supply the 'occupier' i.e. the person living there with or without the deeds of the property being in their name - with such domestic services as –
Gas - (GAS ACT (1986) Section 10(2)),
Electric - (ELECTRICITY ACT (1989) Section 16(1)) and
Water - (WATER INDUSTRY ACT (1991) Section 52(5)).

Thus in R V SECRETARY OF STATE FOR THE ENVIRONMENT EX P DAVIES (1990) it was conceded that a person paying these bills with proof of physical occupancy had further evidence supporting a claim for possession.

Therefore payment of taxes and utilities etc – if linked to actual physical possession of the property – can be supportive evidence.

8) STORAGE

TRELOAR V NUTE (1977) – The storage of materials – wood and stone in this case – were deemed as lending no weight in itself as, in this case, it did not meddle with the enjoyment of the land or exclude the paper owner.

However

If the area had been fenced and then used as a storage area the storage would have been supportive evidence of possession i.e. continual 'use' of the land now under exclusive control.

9) ERECTING NOTICES

This is seen as strong indication of possession but only in certain circumstances. Otherwise it is of little importance.

POWELL V MCFARLANE (1977) ruled that notices, followed by actual enforcements, were a drastic act amounting to possession.

However

The mere erection of signs alone i.e. with no attempt to enforce them, was not enough as in MARSDEN v MILLER (1992) or SIMPSON V FERGUS (1999)

10) CUTTING TREES, TURF OR GRASS

Is often regarded as very weak evidence.

However

In cases where the only use for the land in question was tree cutting, turf or grass cutting the Courts have reached different conclusions for obvious reasons.

For example in the TYRWHITT V WYNNE (1819) case the Court took the sensible and pragmatic view.

The case involved 1,000 acres of mountain land. It was not practical to 'fence in' and 'exclude all others' from such an area and that the cutting and taking of timber was the only real use for that region and therefore doing such constituted ownership.

In WALLIS'S CAYTON BAY HOLIDAY CAMP LTD V SHELL-MEX & BP LTD (1975) cutting grass/silage were deemed to be the only use for the land so that level of possession was the appropriate amount to constitute ownership.

Similarly in CADIJA UMMA V DON MANIS APPU (1939) the cutting of grass was deemed the 'only advantage accruing from the land.'

In WILSON V MARTIN'S EXECUTORS (1993) the Court of Appeal argued that cutting timber might qualify depending on the extent and other use of the land.

In ADAMS V TRUSTEES OF MICHAEL BATT CHARITABLE TRUST (2001). It was held that two cuts of hay a year in an area (which was also fenced off) did constitute ownership and use.

In SEDDON V SMITH (1877) the Judge stated, that 'enclosures', i.e. fencing, walls etc did not always matter. He agreed it was the; "… strongest possible evidence." but noted this particular case was based on land which was ploughed and planted but never enclosed. The individual facts of this particular case proved that this was the 'standard' historical costume/

practice for this type of land in that region and therefore possession with intent was clearly displayed within an area that could be clearly defined despite lack of formal fencing etc.

In NEILSON V POOLE (1969) grass mowing – if it left a distinct line between two 'open' boundaries - could be seen as evidence of acts of ownership to that plot of land.

However

Tree sprawl i.e. branches growing onto another's land was not possession as in LEMMON V WEBB (1895).

Nor was merely collecting fallen wood as in GROSE V WEST (1816) or WILSON V MARTIN'S EXECUTORS (1993)

Indeed cutting grass, tress or turf etc are not considered as acts of possession as they do not have the intent to possess but to 'profit a prende' (Take advantage rather than take possession.) – Courts have been consistent in this view.

In CONVEY V REGAN (1952) the cutting of turf was not deemed possession on its own strength.

In WEST BANK ESTATES LTD V ARTHUR (1967) the irregular cultivation or use of land was deemed not inconsistent with the 'paper owners' enjoyment and the claim failed.

In BOOSEY V DAVIS (1987) the clearing of land of slight scrub was also deemed insufficient.

In COBHAM V FRETT (2001) the occasional incursion onto and acts upon an area just beyond an unfenced boundary were also deemed insufficient for ownership based on control and exclusion of others.

11) GRAZING

Often deemed as poor evidence.

Again this is treated as taking advantage rather than taking possession. In A-G V REES (1859) - LITTLEDALE V LIVERPOOL COLLEGE (1900) and KYNOCH LTD V ROWLANDS (1912) grazing was deemed as unworthy of serious consideration in its own right. The Courts have been consistent in this outlook.

However

In TYRWHITT V WYNNE (1819) and WALLIS'S CAYTON BAY HOLIDAY CAMP LTD V SHELL-MEX & BP LTD (1975) grazing/grass cutting were considered, in these cases, to be strong evidence of possession as the land had little other use.

12) PLAY & RECREATION AREAS

Not regarded as strong evidence of possession.

In TECBILD LTD V CHAMBERLAND (1969), NEWLANDS (CHARMOUTH) LTD V LANGRAN (1989) and DEAR V WOODS (1984) letting children play on 'open ground' (not fenced etc) are unimportant as evidence when making an Adverse Possession claim.

In TRELOAR V NUTE (1977) use by motorcycles on 'open ground' were also deemed to have little weight. These sorts of acts were again deemed as taking advantage rather than taking possession.

In DEAR V WOODS (1984) the dumping of rubbish, playing of children and few perambulations by the squatter were not deemed 'possession'

In NEWLANDS CHARMOUTH LTD V LANGRAN (1989) a 'bramble' hedge was grown and this separated the true owners' garden – the squatter maintained the rough patch behind the bramble hedge and used it for a child's play area and for fires. She lost the case as she knew and accepted the land was actually owned by the neighbour and she had made no effort to exclude them.

The use of land for even regular walking, hiking, jogging, short cuts, fishing, shooting etc, etc or other such activities would almost certainly constitute taking advantage rather than taking possession.

However

In RED HOUSE FARMS V CATCHPOLE (1977) it was deemed shooting on an area of around one acre of swamp/marsh was the only real use for the land so the claim for possession was valid.

Thus teamed with other evidence i.e. exclusion of others to the property and the practising of such activates as described above on the land may be considered supporting evidence.

i.e. In WARREN v YOELL (1944) the area was fenced of and used as a play area – this was deemed ownership as there was complete enclosure and the 'play' was deemed further evidence of exclusive use.

13) GRANTING LEASES ETC, EMPLOYEES, AGENTS AND OTHER SPECIAL RELATIONSHIPS

Is 'killer' evidence in an Adverse Possession claim as it shows a Landlord leased, rented or formed some other sort of 'special relationship'/agency with the squatter. This removes the illegality of possession, which means it is simply no longer adverse.

In BRISTOW V CORMICAN (1878) it was deemed that such a relationship was 'clear and distinct evidence' of the paper owner's superior rights against the squatter. The Courts enforce this rule vigorously.

However

In ALSTON & SONS LTD V BOCM CHEMICALS LTD (2009) ASTON from 1974 to 1977 had farmed agricultural land rent free on the basis that the owner could have it back when required. ALSTON carried on farming the land after 1977 and it was ruled that he had done so without objection or comment from the owner however this amounted to acquiescence (by adverse possession) and not implied permission.

Thus it would now seem age old tool for defeating adverse possession claims – it was not adverse possession but implied consent - is now to be defined very, very narrowly – the 'special relationship' must be clearly definable. (Please see the section on '**AGENTS**' for further details.)

14) LOCAL COSTUME/HISTORICAL FACTORS

These will be judged on a case-by-case basis and may prove to be highly relevant or meaningless.

In SEDDON V SMITH (1877) the Judge stated, that 'enclosures', i.e. fencing, walls etc did not always matter. He agreed it was the; "… strongest possible evidence." but noted this particular case was based on land which was ploughed and planted but never enclosed. The individual facts of this particular case proved that this was the 'standard' historical costume/practice for this type of land in that region and therefore possession with intent was clearly displayed within an area that could be clearly defined despite lack of formal fencing etc.

In brief the claim for Adverse Possession succeeded as the historical/costume based facts of that region in this particular case supported the claim. This may not always be the case.

15) ELECTORAL REGISTER

In KING v JOB (2002) it was held that the Judge was correct to hold registration on the ELECTORAL ROLL as evidence of residence. The Electoral Roll or Electoral

Register as it is often called is a UK government held database for all registered voters at their home addresses. It is also used by many financial institutions to verify your identity and by credit reference agencies to compile credit reports on 'registered' occupants. It is therefore logical that it is deemed good evidence in Adverse Possession cases.

SUMMARY

Again it must be noted that the above topics are not in any form of standardised or accepted table as there is no such table. They are loose generalisations of repetitive Case Law explained in a reasonably practical and easily referenced way which explains that each case is completely dependent upon its own facts.

PRACTICAL EXERCISE

From the breakdown of evidence above a reader should be able to pick out the relevant circumstances of most individual cases and ascertain what evidence amounts to strong, weak, supportive or insignificant.

For example

'Made up' Case A

Mr A has closed of a 3-acre field. He has grown trees to two sides of the property. Built a wall and fence to one side and built an earth dike and ditch to the remaining side. He has constructed a gate and chained/padlock it. Installed a shed for tools and animal feed storage. He has erected 'keep out' signs along the edge of the field that borders the road and has evidence that he has 'hunted' people who have tried or actually entered the property. Each year he rotates the field between crop and grazing cattle. From late autumn to mid spring the field sits idle.

From the above you could pick out individual Case Law that would amount to Mr A having a very strong case for Adverse Possession. He has clearly secured all the borders of the property and controlled access via a locked gate. He has put up 'keep out' warning signs and enforced them by removing anyone he finds breaching these boundaries. He has constructed a shed. He uses the land to grow crops one year and graze cattle the next year. The land may be idle for several months of the year but this is customary to 'barn' animals in winter and crops will not grow in winter so the land is used as is customary/practical.

'Made up' Case E

Mrs E has fenced in an area at the bottom of her garden. It is very marshy and is left as is. Eventually people break through the hedge and use the area as a short cut. Mrs E puts up 'no entry' signs and tries to enforce them. She frequently attempts to block the holes in the hedge but these are frequently vandalised.

From the above you could pick out Case Law which indicate Mrs E's use of the land - - i.e. leaving it as a marsh is the only practical use for the land. E is trying as best as she might to exclude all others by turning away any trespassers she catches and by maintaining the fence in efforts to achieve full and exclusive control of the property and therefore has a very reasonable case for Adverse Possession

'Made up' Case L

Mrs L is claiming possession to 150 acres of rough hilly land. She claims to have used it for minor forestry. She has a very small herd of 33 cows but these are mostly kept close to a small house she has built on the property.

In this case we can be less certain of a decision. Building a home, logging and grazing can be seen as strong evidence of possessing rough terrain as fencing in such a quantity of land would be deemed an unlikely event. However the fact the cows are limited to an almost fixed area and that the evidence of the foresting seems inadequate might suggest a lack of control of the entire region. More detail of the area and the persons use of it would be required.

EVIDENCE – ACKNOWLEDGEMENTS AS EVIDENCE

Acknowledgements are any forms of information passed between the two opposing parties.

Acknowledgements are mostly kept to 'written statements' or judgements on 'actions' actually carried out in reference to the property by the squatter, paper owner or their verified agents. The Courts are wary of '3rd party' influences. They also have a distaste for verbal evidence from either party. In Bolton MBC v Musa (1998) pointed out "... such self serving evidence is hardly ever likely to be of assistance."

Statements (Acknowledgements) should relentlessly support ones own position. If you are the squatter in possession you should always refer to yourself as the 'true owner' due to possession and make no conciliatory noises. If you are the actual 'paper owner' you should do like wise – all parties are the 'real owner' until the Courts say different.

Failure to express your position clearly and without compromise or exception may result in a squatter or owner defeating his or her own claim.

Under the LIMITATION ACT (1980) SECTION 29 (2) acknowledgement must be made by the person in possession (or their authorised agent/s) to the paper owner (or his authorised agent/s) or vice versa. Such statements to, or from, any other '3rd parties' are of no effect.

In LUCAS V DENNISON (1843) and BATCHELOR V MIDDLETON (1948) it was deemed that 3rd party acknowledgements/statements were not to be regarded. (See the 'ORAL' section below for reasons behind such logic.)

After the limitation period has expired no acknowledgement will have any effect (As time has run out) as set in the LIMITATION ACT (1980) SECTION 29 (7)

In all cases it would be extremely wise to retain ones stance as 'true owner.' without ever expressing consolatory overtones. Never refer to yourself as the 'squatter', 'adverse possessor' or any other term other than 'Owner.'

Written & Signed
Acknowledgements/statements must be 'written.' They must also be signed by person making the statement. If not they will have no effect under the LIMITATION ACT (1980) SECTION 29.

Under SECTION 30 of the same ACT an agent also making such 'written' acknowledgements also counts as evidence.

EXCEPTIONS – 'WITHOUT PREJUDICE' STATEMENTS

In the case of OFULUE (and another) V BOSSERT (2008)

It was judged that a squatter marking correspondence 'without prejudice' meant that any acknowledgement to the paper owners' entitlement within that correspondence could not be submitted as evidence. This upholds the legal tradition of permitting preliminary but none committal 'bargaining' which has no legal status.

Therefore a true owner or squatter who wanted to speak freely in the interest of clarifying matters it would be wise to mark all communication as _**Without Prejudice**_ at the very outset of the said communication.

Oral

Under SECTION 29 of THE LIMITATION ACT (1980) 'oral' acknowledgements are not effective

However in HOBBS V WADE (1887) an oral acknowledgement can be used in evidence to show the necessary facts but may not carry any more weight than 'he said, she said, I said, he said, she said' evidence.

In BROWNE V PERRY (1991) – on oral admissions the PRIVY COUNCIL ruled that in such bitter disputes - as those over property - often led to a strong pressure for "oral misrepresentation" – the 'he said, she said, he said, I said, he said, she said' game would run rampant and would become all to common. Writing would prevent and finalise such situations – "There is no room for fraud, mistake or failure of memory. The written word speaks for itself."

The same point was underlined in the LAW REFORMS COMMITTEE'S 21st REPORT ON THE FINAL LIMITATION OF ACTIONS CMND 6923 (1977) PARAGRAPH 2.65 which stated 'temptation' and conflicts of oral evidence were a dangerous place to go and should be mostly avoided.

What is writing?
Under the INTERPRETATION ACT (1978) SCHEDULE 1 'writing' pretty much includes all forms and modes of representing letters and words – typing, email, hand writing, faxes photography, printing, lithography etc, etc.

Indeed the type of documents that can contain acknowledgment/evidence are virtually limitless and at the discretion of the Courts – Financial accounts, pleadings, witness statements, requests for information or further information, affidavits, wills and any other information can be considered.

In FLYNN V FLYNN (1969) The document must be viewed in the circumstances in which it was made and taken as a whole document – taking out 'suitable extracts' and ignoring the overall drive of the information was not permitted as ruled in SURRENDRA OVERSEAS LTD V GOVERNMENT OF SRI LANKA (1977).

Signature and date.
A signature (Or initials will do – ST JOHN V
BOUGHTON (1838)

Can appear anywhere on the document - HOLMES V
MARKRELL (1858)
&
If one document refers to another the one signature on
either/any of them will normally cover all the items that
can be 'read together' - BYRNLEA PROPERTY
INVESTMENTS LTD V RAMSEY (1969)

The date is normally not that important as extrinsic
aids can prove the relevant time frame in most
instances - EDMUNDS V DOWNES (1834)

EVIDENCE – IMPLIED ACKNOWLEDGEMENT

The LAW REFORM COMMITTEES 21ST REPORT ON THE FINAL LIMITATION OF ACTIONS CMND 6923 conceded 'implied' was a tricky scenario and refused to become involved in defining what implied meant in statutory/legal terms.

However in some cases it is obvious what was implied. If a squatter writes to an owner asking to rent the property or asking for repairs etc it is obvious that the paper owners' ownership is being conceded even though it is not being directly referred to. In EDGINTON V CLARK (1964). The squatter writing and asking to purchase the property was deemed as a confession to the true owners' rights.

In LAMBETH LONDON BOROUGH COUNCIL V BIDGEN (2000) squatters writing to the Council requesting that they did not sell the property amounted to admission that the Council was the true owner with the right to actually sell it.

In LAMBETH LONDON BOROUGH COUNCIL V ARCHANGEL (2002) the squatter wrote the words '…used in refurbishing Lambeth's property.' When applying for financial aid. This was deemed an admission of the Councils better title.

However

In ZARB AND ANOTHER V PARRY AND ANOTHER (2011) in 1992 a portion of the disputed property was offered to and bought by the defendants - who also occupied the adjoining property. The dispute over this remaining adjoining property broke out again in 2007 when the claimants entered the remaining land which the defendants still controlled. The claimants tried to erect a fence and did cut down a tree only to be challenged and removed by the defendants. The judge ruled the sale did not start time running afresh and the more recent entry by the claimants was not sufficient to regain control of the area to which the defendants had and still retained control over.

In DOE D CRUZON V EDMONS (1840) It was also ruled that a letter which does not imply or admit 'superior ownership' cannot be used against the person writing it. In this case a letter to rent land stated; "Although, if matters were contested, I am of the opinion that I should establish a legal right to the premises." The letter then went on to agree to rent the land in question. The judge rightly deemed the letter was hardly an admission of better title to any other party. (However renting the land would certainly been seen as such an admission.)

In BREE V SCOTT (1904) Bargaining between the two parties which never admits superior ownership even when, as in KLEANTHONS V LONDON BOROUGH OF BARNET (2006) this bargaining resulted in an offer being made to end the dispute out of court were also deemed to be no admission of 'better title.'

<u>I will repeat again - one should retain their 'true owner' position in no uncertain terms, at all times, on all occasions and even when taking advantage of the 'without prejudice' rule noted above.</u>

EVIDENCE – OTHER COMPLICATIONS

OTHER ILLEGALITY AND
ADVERSE POSSESSION

As previously stated all Adverse Possession must be illegal – for a start you are - by error or design - somewhere you are 'legally' not entitled to be and you will also have every intention to remain.

As also already noted trespass is a civil wrong. Trespass followed by actual continual possession removes the ability of the paper owner to sue the possessor for trespass or to request removal of their presence. Indeed possession turns the tables in the squatters favour.

However other illegal acts which contravene criminal law mostly act as evidence for Adverse Possession and the fact criminal punishment may be due to the squatter does not alter the claim for Adverse Possession – crime really does pay in certain circumstances.

In ADVOCATE V (1880) the HOUSE OF LORDS pointed out that using illegal fishing nets and breaches of the law in this claim actually provided evidence in the squatters favour – "its illegality does not make it the less an important element in shewing what the possession was. ... That whether legal or not, is perfect possession..."

In LAMBETH LONDON BOROUGH COUNCIL V BLACKBURN (2001) the squatter was honest enough to admit he broke in by cutting a padlock – a criminal offence under the CRIMINAL DAMAGE ACT (1971) SECTION 1(1) – any argument to prevent Adverse Possession based on this fact was deemed pointless and not even lodged as a technicality.

Thus illegality is always required in cases of Adverse Possession and acts of further illegality can often be supportive of such behaviour.

TIME & ADVERSE POSSESSION

In England and Wales this will revolve around a 12-year time limit for **unregistered** land as established in THE LIMITATION ACT (1980) SECTION 15 (1) (It also includes **registered** land where 12 + years Adverse Possession has already been obtained by 25th February 2002.)

Or

10 or 12 year time limit for registered land under THE LAND REGISTRATION ACT (2002). Please note this (2002) ACT comes with a slightly different claims procedure to the LIMITATION ACT (1980) that may result in a ten-year limitation period.

In Scotland the limitation period is 10 years.

In Northern Ireland the limitation period is 12 years on registered and unregistered land.

EXCLUSIONS TO THE ABOVE CONDITIONS

Mines and minerals etc are virtually excluded from Adverse Possession claims -
Coal is covered by the LIMITATION ACT (1980) SECTION 10(2)(a)

Gold and silver by the same ACT - SECTION 37(6)

Petroleum (Oil) by PETROLEUM PRODUCTION
ACT (1934)
Uranium by the ATOMIC ENERGY ACT (1946)

So if, by some miracle you find diamonds or other
such natural 'untapped goodies' on a property you are
claiming Adverse Possession upon you may be very
badly out of luck.

The 'Crown'
The Crown is normally defined as the King/Queens
property or 'persons acting on behalf of the Crown' –
i.e. the DEPARTMENTS OF STATE – (Government
Departments such as the Ministry of Defence,
Ministry of Agriculture etc, etc.)

Such property is covered by the LIMITATION
ACT (1980) SECTION 37

A period of 30 years (For some reason.) applies against
Crown land.

and

60 years if the case involves 'foreshore' (In the UK the
Crown owns almost all the foreshore – basically the
land uncovered between high and low tide.)

Spiritual or Eleemosynary corporations sole
Under the LIMITATION ACT (1980) SCHEDULE

1 PT 2 PARAGRAPHS 10 – 11 sets a 30-year limit on such claims.

Eleemosynary cases are now becoming a thing of the past (Charities who distribute alms or bounty of the charities founder.)

Spiritual 'organisations' are not defined in the ACT but it could be taken to mean all 'official' religions property holdings.

TIME – HOW TO STOP IT RUNNING

The general rule is quite simple – once time starts to run in favour of the Adverse Possessor (squatter) it continues to do so until the paper owner commences and follows through legal action to recover the property or physically retakes the property.

In BENZON RE BOWER V CHETWYND (1914) "… The well established rule that if the Statue begins to run it continues to run whatever happens… The rule may work in hardship in particular cases, but it is so well-establish that no Court would now decline to follow it."

In RHODES V SMETHURST (1840) the fact that the paper owner was 'busy' and claimed he was unable to appoint representation to defend such a claim was wisely deemed by the Judge as stupid - 'I couldn't have been bothered' defence was not sufficient to stop time running.

Equally a paper owner who would be cunning enough to put his property (estate) into 'assurance'- meaning some sort of transfer, sale, lease, mortgage, settlement or other legal 'positioning' - does not effect the fact time has started to run in favour of the person in actual possession - STACKPOOLE V STACKPOOLE (1843).

In SECRETARY OF STATE FOR FOREIGN AND COMMONWEALTH AFFAIRS V TOMLIN (1990) TIMES 4 DECEMBER the Crown 'bought' land *just before* the squatters 12 year period had been fulfilled. The legal status of the new owner (The Crown/ Government.) might have increased the waiting period to 30 years for Crown properties. The conveyance/ transfer of the land to the Crown might also have been judged as being unable to alter the right to a possession period which was already running (i.e. 12 years instead of 30 years) but TOMLIN argued the property was not Crown land and his case failed on this issue leaving the matter of the 'time running anomaly' undecided.

However in THORNTON V FRANCE (1897) the true owner mortgaged a property, which was already being squatted. The Courts supported the squatter's rights over that of those who were party to the mortgage. "... the ACT does not confer a new right of entry on the mortgagee... a man in possession holding adversely to the mortgagor... has already began to run in his favour against the mortgagor."

Thus, the Crown or any other party probably could not increase the length of the limitation from the original position in which the squatter took up possession i.e. the Crown buying land (with a squatter upon it) from a private person would have to accept that the squatters Limitation period would probably still remain at 12 years and a squatter who began possession of Crown land which was then sold to a private individual would have to accept that the Limitation period *might* well remain at the full 30 years. (Or *perhaps* if the Adverse Possessor had under 18 years actual possession when the property was transferred from the Crown he/she would then be in a position to wait a further 12 years to reach the limitation period for a 'normal' Adverse Possession case.)

TIME – EXTENSION FOR MENTAL DISABILITY

Covered by THE LIMITATION ACT (1980) SECTION 28 (1)–(4)

The effect of this provision is to extend the normal limitation period when the paper owner is of 'unsound mind.'

Under SECTION 38 (3) this extension lasts for 6 years from the time the disability ceases (or until the person dies within this period.)

Under the MENTAL HEALTH ACT (1983) the Government can appoint an 'agent' to manage the affairs of a person who is or becomes unsound of mind if a person is not already acting in this capacity for the individual. This agent will be covered by the ACT on the individuals' behalf.

The disability exception only applies if the disability was present *before* the right to claim Adverse Possession arises.

Successive disabilities, which overlap making the 'illness/es' continual, are treated as one disability

regardless of the actual details – see BORROWS V
ELLISON (1871).

A recovery, even for one day, which is then followed by
another illness, will result in the situation described above
under SECTION 38 (3) – i.e. the illness will be deemed
'over' and no further extension will be provided for. See
GOODALL V SKERRATT (1855) or OWEN V DE
BEAUVOIR (1847)/DE BEAUVOIR V OWEN (1850)

If illness occurs one day after that date which a claim
for adverse possession could be made it will not prevent
the claim from being valid. See - GOODALL V
SKERRATT (1855) or MURRAY V WATKINS (1980)

Were one owner (with a mental disability) dies and
leaves it to another with a mental disability it will have
no effect on the squatters right to claim and the second
persons disability will not be considered under the
LIMITATION ACT (1980).

A 'squatter's' mental capacity or age is not considered if
they are in actual possession it is not deemed relevant
to the case.

TIME - EXTENSION FOR MINORS

Covered by THE LIMITATION ACT (1980)
SECTION 28 (1)-(4)

Under SECTION 38 (3) this extension lasts for 6 years
from the age of consent (or until the person dies within
this period.)

The effect of this provision is to extend the normal limitation period when the paper owner is a minor – i.e. a person currently aged 17 or under.

Since 1962 (LAW OF PROPERTY ACT (1925) SECTION 1(6) and LAND REGISTRATION ACT (1925) SECTION 3 (IV) it has been impossible for a minor (currently aged 17 or under) to legally own 'estate property' (land, house etc.) An adult acting as his/her agent holds this in his trust.

This agent can avail of these provisions of the ACT on the minors' behalf.

TIME - EXTENSION FOR FRAUD

Under the LIMITATION ACT (1980) SECTION 32 the start date of the claim period can be extended due to fraud/deliberate concealment.

Such cases in Adverse Possession are rare so this topic would seem to be an unimportant issue.

In fraud/deliberate concealment cases the 'start time' then becomes the point when this situation could, or with reasonable attention, should have been noticed as underlined in SHELDON V RHM OUTHWAITE (1996) case.

These exclusions do not apply to an innocent '3rd party' – THE LIMITATION ACT 1920 section 32(3) and (4) - who acquired rights form and then 'stepped into' such a situation left by the original squatter without knowing the full extent of the situation - as the new possessor was not deliberately concealing or mistaken in their understanding of the situation they have not committed fraud. It was deemed that any previous concealment will not affect the new and 'innocent' squatters' right and he/she can add the 'concealing successors' time to their own Adverse Possession claim as established in EDDIS V CHICHESTER CONSTABLE (1969).

However if the 'concealment' was known the new party was not innocent and the normal rules for fraud applied. See VANE V VANE (1873)

In KING V VICTOR PARSONS & CO (1973) (At 33) –

'Knowingly' (Knows it is wrong.)

Or

'Recklessly' (Considers or should have noticed doing something could be wrong but carries on regardless.)

Were the two terms used to establish if a party should be (or should not be) liable for such a limitation period extension i.e. –

In VANE V VANE (1873) where a child was deliberately (Knowingly) passed off as the legitimate heir and in CHETHAM v HOARE (1870) the deeds were (Recklessly) destroyed.

It is important to note fraud or deliberate concealment and secretly trying to possess land quite rightly fails to meet the 'open and honest' possession required to make a claim. You may not want, or feel the need, to strike up a marching band and set off fire works to draw attention to a possession, you may even treasure your privacy and enjoy the quite life but to wilfully and deliberately conceal possession is treated dimly.

DISCOVERY OF CONCEALMENT

Reasonable diligence towards such discovery was discussed in PECO ARTS INC V HAZLITT GALLERY LTD (1983) (A case not related to Adverse Possession.) To generalise and convert this 'due diligence' into Adverse Possession cases it would be fair to state that occasionally inspecting ones property/possession would suffice i.e. every few years a patrol of your possession followed by taking action / removing all 'intruders' if required. (See the SOLLING v BROUGHTON (1893) case for a factual example.)

In PUDRICK V LONDON BOROUGH OF HACKNEY (2003) the adverse possessor "... was keeping his head down... he was [not] doing anything dishonest or underhand; he was not lying to the council or its representatives; he was not denying to anyone that he was in occupation... There is no question of Mr. P being guilty of any fraud or deliberate concealment..."

Indeed refusing to draw attention to an Adverse Possession is a sensible approach – "An owner of property who makes no use of it, whatever, should be expected to keep an eye on property... A period of 12 years is a long period during which to neglect a property completely." It is not for the Adverse Possessor to warn them of such neglect especially when they are taking full advantage of it.

This was approved in TOPPLAN ESTATES LTD V TOWNLEY (2005) "... I can see no basis for the suggestion that the fact that the respondent did not protest, or attempt to prevent the county's workmen from appropriating the road strip... means he did not intend to continue his factual possession... the respondent's conduct in 'lying low'... in my judgement... there can be no obligation in law on a squatter to draw the true owners attention to the fact that time is running against him..."

Attention can be drawn to the fact that T was not acting fraudulently. He was acting diplomatically. He did not challenge the council over its use of part of the land. He did not provoke them into possibly taking action against his possession. He assumed they were not there to assert permanent possession. He kept a low profile in the hope they would leave him in peace – this they eventually did.

It was agreed that in such situations each case would rest on its own facts and would revolve around the actions which an 'ordinary person' would have conducted when they had 10 or 12 years to secure their interests in a property.

TIME - EXTENSION FOR MISTAKE

Mistakes are not relevant and will not stop time running in the favour of the possessor regardless of what the ACT actually states. Case law has firmly established that 'possession' by mistake or deliberate intentions have the same end result – time runs in favour of the possessor and their claim is still valid.

Thus if I sell you my house and the drive is around 20 meters wide between me and my neighbour – this is what you and I believe we have traded. However the Neighbour discovers the fence should be 2 meters towards my house – a 'mistake' has been made and can be remedied by moving the fence to the correct place.

However this does not affect the Adverse Possession situation i.e.

If the fence had been in place for *over* the limitation period an Adverse Possession claim would probably succeed.

If it had been in place for *under* the limitation period but regardless of the neighbours silence or objections, was allowed to remain for that period of time an Adverse Possession claim would still probably succeed.

If the neighbour took action and carried it through to its conclusion the claim would most likely fail.

TIME - SUSPENDING OTHER REASONS

Several other things can 'suspend' time -

WAR
During a war whilst the necessary party is detained in enemy territory, is in action or is the enemy (See LIMITATION (ENEMIES AND WAR PRISONERS) ACT (1945)

LEGAL ACTIONS

The commencement of a legal action to recover land will not stop time from running. If such an action is started - but not pursued to enforcement of the Judgement for what ever reason – i.e. struck out, delayed or in any way abandoned – it does not effect the ticking of the clock.

In MARKFIELD INVESTMENTS LTD V EVANS (2001) the issue of a writ etc in earlier proceedings is no more relevant than a simple verbal demand for possession – the legal action threatened by the writ etc must be followed through or it is meaningless.

In MOUNT CARMEL LTD V PETER THURLOW LTD (1988) such a demand did "…not start time running afresh… otherwise all the true owner would have to do to avoid Adverse Possession claims is issue a writ every twelve years without more."

The fact a Judgement has been reached also does not stop time running providing the squatter still remains in possession as the Judgement is not enforced – see HAMILTON V R (1917) (Canadian case.)

In short all the legal action an owner pleases can be taken and all of it can succeed in the Court room but if the paper owner doesn't enforce these Judgements and the squatter sits tight to beyond the limitation period – the papers owners case is in trouble.

However legal action might have the effect of extending the limitation period in certain circumstances. (See **'WILLING CONFUSION ABOUT TIME LIMITS'** section to follow for more details on such matters.)

TIME - WILLING CONFUSION ABOUT LIMITS - ENFORCING A JUDGEMENT ALREADY ACHIEVED BEFORE THE POSSESSOR REACHES THE REQUIRED LIMITATION PERIOD.

This topic is full of nonsense. The language of 'legal excrement' has been spoken fluently and dripped all over it. In effect, legal action against the squatter, before the limitation period has passed can extend the actual length of Adverse Possession required.

Legally speaking there is no limit on the enforcement of a judgement once it has been obtained. (i.e. a judgement to remove the squatter from the property.) However if it is not enforced within 6 years (COUNTY COURT PRACTICE 1 46.2 (a)/SCHEDULE 2) the person possessing the Judgement must ask for 'leave of the Court.' Upon which the Court will review the reasons for any extension and almost always automatically reject such a request.

In BP PROPERTIES LTD V BUCKLER (1987) a 'retake the property' Judgement was obtained before the 12 year limitation period required by the squatter but not enforced until after that period.

The COURT OF APPEAL stated that the 'action to retake possession' was valid for enforcement for a further 12 years after its issue date as contained in the LIMITATION ACT (1939) SECTION 2 (4) – in short the enforcement extended the limitation time on an Adverse Possession by 12 more years (A total of nearly 24 years.) in favour of a paper owner who took action *before* the original 12 year, 'squatting' period had expired.

This anomaly was then inherited by the LIMITATION ACT (1980) SECTION 24 (1) but halved the period to enforce an action to retake possession to 6 years provided this action began *before* the squatter had possession for the normal 12 year period – in effect extending the limitation period to nearly 18 years.

This obviously created confusion - Was there a 12 years Adverse Possession limit or could a paper owner extend it to potentially another 6 or even 12 years over the limitation period?

The COURT OF APPEAL in the LOUGHER V DONOVAN (1948) case had the Judge rule that the 12 year limit (set under the LIMITATION ACT (1939)) to enforce a judgement was the maximum allowed for any enforcement if issued *before* the squatter had reached the 12 year limitation period.

However another division of the COURT OF APPEAL came to the opposite view in LAMB & SONS V RIDER (1948). Here it was ruled that there was no time limit on the enforcement of judgements obtained *before* the squatter had reached the limitation period.

In NATIONAL WESTMINSTER BANK PLC V POWNEY (1991) it was pointed out these two positions could not be justified. It argued LOUGHER V DONOVAN (1948) was wrong.

The Judges argued LAMB & SONS V RIDER (1984) was correct but only if the Courts had a 'discretion' to enforce the judgement - *a discretion which would always be refused.*

Thus under the COUNTY COURT PRACTICE ORDER 26 RULE 5 the person seeking enforcement of an 'order' over 6 years old must ask for 'leave of the Court.' Upon which the Court will review the reasons for the extension and almost always automatically reject such a request - unless it could be found the Court was to blame for the delay.

Hence, to summarise, if legal action is successfully taken - via the Courts - to remove the squatter *before* the limitation period for an Adverse Possession claim has passed this action can grant the paper owner a further 6 years to evict the adverse possessor. (A total of nearly 18 years.)

This confusion over enforcement times may be 're-born' due to the passing of THE LAND REGISTRATION ACT (2002) PART 9 SECTION 98 which covers registered land in England and Wales. This ACT in effect grants not 12 or 6 but a 2 year 'enforcement' extension to remove the squatter.

"(2) A judgment for possession of land ceases to be enforceable at the end of the period of 2 years beginning with the date of the judgment..."

"(4) A judgment for possession of land ceases to be enforceable at the end of the period of 2 years beginning with the date of the judgment if, at the end of that period, the person against whom the judgment was given is entitled to make an application under paragraph 6 of Schedule 6 to be registered as the proprietor of an estate in the land."

EVICTION

I must point out that tens of thousands of homes, other buildings and endless acres of land have been left to the elements. Programmes such as the BBC's 'Britain's Empty Homes' openly show councils up and down the nation trying to stall the problem via Empty Dwelling Management Orders or Compulsory Purchase Orders.

These properties are a blight, health hazard and a pure waste of limited resources. It is with regard to these properties I have a great deal of sympathy for the true 'civilised adverse possessor' taking possession and making good and neighbourly use.

This book is about Adverse Possession and therefore does not cover eviction or the process and resistance to that process. One will also find solicitors much more 'friendly' and educated in such matters as eviction. With Landlord/tenant disputes and mortgage repossession procedures these cases are all too common. SEEK LEGAL ADVICE for such a complicated topic.

Arming ones self with the basic concepts of the topic is also a wise decision.

If you are *not* evicted by section 7 of THE CRIMINAL LAW ACT (1977) (Amended by THE CRIMINAL JUSTICE & PUBLIC ORDER ACT 1994) - the paper owner must use the 'civil' Court process to apply for a possession order to have you removed

PART 55 of THE CIVIL PROCEDURE RULES (1998 amended 2008) is the 'tool of eviction' used in almost all cases to remove you from all property – house, land, flat etc, etc and is used by almost everyone who would evict you, paper owner, mortgage company etc, etc.

Details of this procedure and defences to it are well outside the scope of this book however -

PAGE 48 – 74 of the 'book' published by the ADVISORY SERVICE FOR SQUATTER - SQUATTERS HANDBOOK 2004 12TH EDITION - PAGE 48 – 74 describes PART 55 of THE CIVIL PROCEDURE RULES and how to handle the process.

(The guide is about 80, A5 size pages priced at exceptionally reasonable £1.50) and provides practical and very detailed information on squatting and the practical implications of the law surrounding such, along with a considerable amount of other advice on all aspects of *responsible* squatting. (Unfortunately the service also has a darker side and is often, rightly, accused of lending itself to the parasitic squatters intents.)

It points out that - in brief – the law provides 'due process' - You have a right not to be evicted unless by that proper legal procedure. It states this is now the only real 'squatters' right.' In modern UK (p12) and this eviction must be handled via PART 55 of THE CIVIL PROCEDURE RULES.

If the police or another party try to remove you by cunning, threats or actual violence it is an offence under SECTION 6 of the CRIMINAL LAW ACT (1977) – no individual or party can force entry whilst being opposed - They are like 'vampires' – if you do not invite them in they are not permitted to enter. So refuse their 'charms' quote your legal right - that you cannot be evicted without 'legal due process' and ask them to leave or face a fine of up to £5,000 and /or up to 6 months imprisonment.

Paper owners should also note that the process might be downright frustrating and costly but it is required as illegal acts are not the way ahead. Not only can the CRIMINAL LAW ACT (1977) be used against you but THE PROTECTION OF EVICTION ACT (1977) & HOUSING ACT (1988) also makes it an offence to harass or evict an 'occupier' who (if evicted) can claim damages under a civil tort (civil action) depending on how much the Landlord gained from the eviction. Or if harassed by the proper owner by applying to the HIGH COURT under the COUNTY COURTS ACT (1984) for an injunction to have the behaviour stopped on pains of legal punishment for the property owner if he/she does not.

Unfortunately this creates a legal state where the *parasitic* squatter who 'enters' and tries to remain in people's private homes – even second homes - are treated far too kindly by the law and bring nothing but disrepute to the true, responsible civilised adverse possessors who make good use of permanently abandoned property.

STEVE BIRD reporting for the DAILY MAIL (DAILY MAIL, Saturday, September 10, 2011) cites a figure of 20,000 squatted properties in the UK. (Without verifying the source or distinguishing between 'civilised' or 'parasitic squatters'.)

In the case of parasitic squatters I completely believe that private paper owners should be entitled to have their properties legally protected from 'entry without consent or without ongoing consent,' They should not face a lengthy, extremely costly and nerve wrecking civil legal process which they must fund themselves whilst the authorities protect this rancid little type of 'grubby squatter' and even provide them with legal aid - where the Government – or should I say the tax payer - pays their legal fees - to further extend the proper owners misery.

This type of disgusting parasitic squatting is nothing but vicious and cruel. It is completely criminal in all but name. It is a hideous practice to invade a person's home and try to remain by using the law to draw out the process for as long as possible until legally evicted, at great effort to the owner who may now have been left homeless along with his/her family – they will also be a lot poorer for such cases are far from cheap. This practice gives true 'civilised' squatting – taking adverse possession of an unwanted property for societies betterment – a very bad name.

I hope the new laws - promised by Justice Secretary for State Clarke in late 2010 - to end the grubby squatters activities of occupying a private properties are passed into statue quickly. I also hope these new more stringent laws offer a fairer balance to landlords in relation to tenants who lapse paying rent thereby becoming the parasitic type of squatter.

But enough of my rantings ☺

ADVERSE POSSESSION – CASE REFERENCES

ADAMS v TRUSTEES OF MICHAEL BATT CHARITABLE
TRUST 2001
82 P & CR 406, 2001 21 EG 164 CS, SUB NOM

ADVOCATE v BLANTYRE 1879
4 APP CAS 770, HL

ADVOCATE v LOVAT 1880
5 APP CAS 273, HL

A-G v REES 1859
23 JP 308, 4 DE G & J 55, 5 JUR NS 745, 7 WR 404,
33 LTOS 189

AG SECURITIES v VAUGHAN 1990
1 AC 417, 1988 1 EGLR 36, 1988 7 LS GAZ R 39, 1988 3 WLR
1205, 57 P & CR 17, 21 HLR 79, 1988 2 EGLR 78, 1989 1 LS
GAZ R 39, 1988 47 EG 193, HL

AGENCY CO LTD (TRUSTEES & EXECUTORS) v SHORT 1888
13 APP CAS 793, 53 JP 132, 58 LJCP 4, 37 WR 433, 59 LT 677,
4 TLR 736, PC

ALLAN v LIVERPOOL OVERSEERS 1874
LR 9 QB 180

ALLEN v ENGLAND 1862
3 F & F 49

ASHE (TRUSTEE IN BANKRUPTCY OF DJABAR BADAI)
v NATIONAL WESTMINSTER BANK PLC 2008
EWCA CIV 55 2008 WLR D 40

ASHER v WHITLOCK 1865
LR 1 QB 1, 30 JP 6, 35 LJQB 17, 11 JUR NS 925, 14 WR 26,
13 LT 254

BAMPTON v BURCHALL 1842
5 BEAV 67

BASILDON DISTRICT COUNCIL v CHARGE 1996
CLY 4929

BATCHELOR v MIDDLETON 1848
6 HARE 75, 8 LTOS 513

BENZON RE BOWER v CHETWYND 1914
2 CH 68, 83 LJ CH 658, 21 MANS 8, 58 SOL JO 430,
110 LT 926, 30 TLR 435, CA

BEVAN v LONDON PORTLAND CEMENT CO LTD 1892
3 R 47, 67 LT 615, 9 TLR 12

BLADDER v PHILLIPS 1991
EGCS 109, CA

BATT V ADAMS 2001
2 EGLR 92, 2001 32 EG 90

BLIGH v MARTIN 1968
1 ALL ER 1157, 1968 1 WLR 804, 19 P & CR 442, 112 SOL JO
189, 206 ESTATES GAZETTE 25

BOOSEY v DAVIS 1987
55 P & CR 83, CA

BORROWS v ELLISON 1871
LR 6 EXCH 128, 40 LJ EX 131, 19 WR 850, 19 WR 850,
24 LT 365

BP PROPERTIES LTD v BUCKLER 1987
55 P & CR 337, 1897 2 EGLR 168, 1987 NLJ REP 899,
284 ESTATES GAZETTE 375, CA

BRISTOW v CORMICAN 1878
3 APP CAS 641, HL

BROWN v PERRY 1991
1 WLR 1297, 64 P & CR 228, 135 SOL JO LB 173, PC

BROWNE v DAWSON 1840
12 AD & EL 624, 10 LJQB 7, ARN & H 114, 4 PER & DAV 355

BUCKINGHAMSHIRE COUNTY COUNCIL v MORAN 1988
86 LGR 472, 56 P & CR 372; AFFD 1990 CH 623, 1989 2 ALL
ER 225, 1989 3 WLR 152, 88 LGR 145, 58 P & CR 236, 1989
NLJR 257, CA

BURROWS v BRENT LONDON BOROUGH COUNCIL 1996
4 ALL ER 577, 1996 1 WLR 1448, 1997 2 FCR 43, 1997 1 FLR
178, 29 HLR 167, 1996 43 LS GAZ R 26, 1996 NLJR 1616, 140
SOL JO LB 239, HL

BYRNLEA PROPERTY INVESTMENTS LTD v RAMSAY 1969
1969 2 QBB 253, 1969 2 WLR 721, 20 P & CR 528, 113 SOL JO
188, 1969 RVR 183, 209 ESTATES GAZETTE 1439, SUB NOM
RE 33, BYRNE ROAD, BALHAM, BYRNLEA PROPERTY
INVESTMENTS V RAMSAY 1969 2 ALL ER 311, CA

CADIJA UMMA v DON MANIS APPU 1939
AC 136, 108 LJPC 13, PC

CARROLL v MANEK & BANK OF INDIA 1999
79 P &CR 173

CAVE v ROBINSON JARVIS AND ROLF 2002
UKHL 18 2002 2 ALL ER 641 2002 2 WLR 1107

CHETHAM v HOARE 1870
LR 9 EQ 571

CHOLMONDELEY v CLINTON 1820
2 JAC & W 1; AFFD 1821 2 JAC & W 189N, 4 BLIGH 1, HL

CHOLMONDELEY v CLINTON 1817
2 MER 171

CLARK v ELPHINSTONE 1880
6 APP CAS 164, 50 LJPC 22 PC, PC

COBHAM v FRETT 2001
1 WLR 1775, 145 SOL JO LB 7, PC

COLCHESTER BOROUGH COUNCIL v SMITH 1991
CH 448, 1991 1 ALL ER 29, 1991 2 WLR 540, 62 P & CR 242;

AFFD 1992 CH 421, 1992 2 ALL ER 561, 1992 2 WLR 728 1992 11 LS GAZ R 32, CA

CONVEY v REGAN 1952
IR 56

COREA v APPUHAMY 1912
AC 230, 81 LJCP 151, 105 LT 836, PC

CRAVEN v PRIDMORE 1902
18 TLR 282, CA

CULLEN v CULLEN 1962
IR 268

CULLEY v DOE D TAYLERSON 1840
11 AD & EL 1008, 9 LJQB 288, 3 PER & DAV 539

CUNLIFFE v LONDON & NORTH WESTERN RLY CO 1888
4 TLR 278, CA

DE BEAUVOIR v OWEN 1850
5 EXCH 166

DEAR v WOODS 1984
CA TRANSCRIPT 318

DES BARRES v SHEY 1873
22 WR 273, 29 LT 592, CR 14 AC 146 ?????

DIXON v GAYFERE 1853
17 BEAV 421, 23 LJ CH 60, 22 LTOS 15

DOE D BAKER v COOMBES 1850
9 CB 714, 19 LJCP 306, 15 LTOS 90

DOE D MILNER v BRIGHTWEN 1809
10 EAST 583

EDDIS v CHICHESTER CONSTABLE 1969
2 CH 345 AT 356–357 CA

EDGINTON v CLARK 1964
1 QB 367, 1963 3 ALL ER 468, 1963 3 WLR 721, 107 SOL JO 617, 187 ESTATES GAZETTE 917, CA

EDMUNDS v DOWNES 1834
2 CR & MN 459, 3 LJ EX 98, 4 TYR 173

EMMANUALE OFULUE & AGNES OFULUE v ERICA
BOSSERT 2008
CA CIV DIV 2008 EWCA CIV 7

EVANS v NA 1873
42 LJ CH 357

FAIRWEATHER v ST MARYLEBONE PROPERTY CO LTD 1963
510, 1962 2 ALL ER 288, 1962 2 WLR 1020, 106 SOL JO 368

FLYNN v FLYNN 1969
2 CH 403, 1969 2 ALL ER 557. 1969 2 WLR 1148,
113 SOL JO 428

FRUIN v FRUIN 1983
CA TRANSCRIPT 448

GOODALL v SKERRATT 1855
3 DREW 216, 24 LJ CH 323, 3 EQ REP 295, 1 JUR NS 57,
3 WR 152, 25 LTOS 6

GROSE v WEST 1816
7 TAUNT 39

HAIGH v WEST 1893
2 QB 19

HAMILTON v R 1917
54 SCR 331, 35 DLR 226

HAWDON v KHAN 1920
20 SRNSW 703 at 707

HOBBS v WADE 1887
36 CH D 553, 57 LJ CH 184, 36 WR 445, 58 LT 9

HOLLINSHEAD v WHEAWALL 1956
167 EG 278

HOLMES v MARKRELL 1858
3 CBNS 789, 30 LTOS 243

HOUNSLOW LONDON BOROUGH COUNCIL v
MINCHINTON 1997
74 P & CR 221, 1997 NPC 44, CA

HUNTER v CANARY WHARF LTD 1994
42 CON LR 22, 1994 INDEPENDANT, 20 DECEMBER; ON
APPEAL 1996 1 ALL ER 482, 1996 2 WLR 348, 28 HLR 383, 47
CON LR 136, 1995 NLJR 1645, 75 BLR 27, 139 SOL JO LB 214,
CA; REVSD 1997 AC 655 1997 2 ALL ER 426, 1997 2 WLR 684,
1997 2 FLR 342, 1997 FAM LAW 601, 30 HLR 409, 1997 19 LS
GAZ R 25, 1997 NLJR 634, 84 BLR 1, 141 SOL JO LB 108, HL

JACK v WALSH 1842
4 ILR 254

JOHN LAING &SONS LTD v KINGSWOOD ASSESSMENT
COMMITTEE 1949
1 KB 344

JOHNSON & SONS LTD v BROCK 1907
2 CH 533, 76 LJ CH 602, 97 LT 294:

JOLLY GATHERCOLE v NORFOLK 1900
2 CH 616, 69 LJ CH 661, 48 WR 657, 1900–3 ALL ER REP 286,
44 SOL JO 642, 83 LT 118, 16 TLR 521, CA

JONES v CHAPMAN 1847
13 JP 730, 18 LJ EX 456, 2 EXCH 803, 14 LTOS 45

KING v VICTOR PARSONS & CO 1973
1 ALL ER 206, 1973 1 WLR 29, 1973 1 LLOYDS REP 189, 116
SOL JO 901, 225 ESTATES GAZETTE 611, CA

KING v JOB 2002
ALL ER D

KIRBY v COWDEROY 1912
AC 599, 81 LJPC 222, 107 LT 74, PC

KYNOCH LTD v ROWLANDS 1912
1 CH 527, 81 LJ CH 340, 106 LT 316, 1911–13 ALL ER REP EXT
1258, CA

LAING & LAING v MORAN & MORAN 1952
2 DLR 468, ONT CA

LAMB (WT) & SONS v RIDER 1948
2 KB 331, 1948 2 ALL ER 402, 1949 LJT 258, 92 SOL JO 556, 64
TLR 530, CA

LAMBETH LONDON BOROUGH COUNCIL v BIGDEN 2000
33 HLR 478, CA

LAMBETH LONDON BOROUGH COUNCIL
v BLACKBURN 2001
EWCA CIV 912, 2001 82 P & CR 494, 33 HLR 847, 2001 26 LS
GAZ R 46, 2001 25 EG 157 CS

LAMBETH LONDON BOROUGH COUNCIL v ARCHANGEL
2002
1 P & CR 230, 33 HLR 490, CA

LEE v PARSONS 1998
6 OCT 1998 UNREPORTED CA

LEIGH v JACK 1879
5 EX D 264, 44 JP 488, 49 LJQB 220, 28 WR 452, 42 LT 463, CA

LEMMON v WEBB 1895
AC 1, 59 JP 564, 64 LJ CH 205, 11 R 116, 1891 - 4 ALL ER REP
749, 71 LT 647, 11 TLR 81, HL

LITTLEDALE v LIVERPOOL COLLEGE 1900
1 CH 19, 69 LJ CH 87, 48 WR 177, 81 LT 564, 16 TLR 44, CA

LOUGHER v DONOVAN 1948
2 ALL ER 11 SUB NOM DONOVAN V LOUGHER 1984 LJR
1383, 92 SOL JO 336, CA

LUCAS v DENNISON 1843
13 SIM 584, 7 JUR 1122, 2 LTOS 186

LUDBROOK v LUDBROOK 19012 KB 96, 70 LJKB 552, 49 WR
465, 45 SOL JO 393, 84 LT 485, 17 TLR 397, CA

LYELL v KENNEDY 1887
18 QBD 796, CA

LYELL v KENNEDY 1889
14 APP CAS 437, 59 LJQB 268, 38 WR 353, 62 LT 77, HL

MAGDALEN HOSPITAL (PRESIDENT & GOVERNORS)
v KNOTTS 1878
8 CH D 709, 47 LJ CH 726, 26 WR 640, 38 LT 624, CA; AFFD
1879 4 APP CAS 324, 43 JP 460, 48 LJ CH 579, 27 WR 602, 40
LT 466, HL

MAGUIRE v MCCLELLANDS CONTRACT 1907
1 IR 393, 41 ILT 182, CA

MANBY v BEWICKE 1857
3 K & J 342, 29 LTOS 276

MARKFIELD INVESTMENTS LTD v EVANS 2001
2 ALL ER 238, 2001 1 WLR 1321, 81 P & CR 473, 81 P & CR
D33, CA

MARSDEN v MILLER 1992
64 P & CR 239, CA

MARSHALL v TAYLOR 1895
1 CH 641, 64 LJ CH 416, 12 R 310, 72 LT 670, CA

MAY v MARTIN 1885
11 VLR 562

MCDONNELL v M'KINTY 1847
10 ILR 514

MORRIS v PINCHES 1969
212 ESTATES GAZETTE 1141

MOUNT CARMEL INVESTMENTS LTD v PETER THURLOW
LTD 1988
3 ALL ER 129, 1988 1 WLR 1078, 57 P & CR 396, 132 SOL JO
1119, CA

MULCAHY v CURRAMORE PTY LTD 1974
2 NSWLR 464

MURRAY v WATKINS 1890
62 LT 796

NATIONAL WESTMINSTER BANK PLC v POWNEY 1991
CH 339, 1990 2 ALL ER 416, 1990 2 WLR 1084, 60 P & CR 420,
134 SOL JO 285, CA

NEILSON v POOLE 1969
20 P & CR 909, 210 ESTATES GAZETTE 113

NEPEAN v DOE D KNIGHT 1837 7
LJ EX 335, 2 M & W 894, MURP & H 291

NESBITT v MABLETHORPE URBAN DISTRICT COUNCIL
1917
2 KB 568, 15 LGR 647, 81 JP 289, 86 LJKB 1401, 117 LT 365;
REVSD 1918 2 KB 1, 16 LGR 313, 82 JP 161, 87 LJKB 705, 118
LT 805, CA

NEWLANDS (CHARMOUTH) LTD v LANGRAN 1989
14 JULY 1989 UNREPORTED CA

NICHOLAS v ANDREWS 1920
20 SR NSW 178

NORTON v LONDON & NORTH WESTERN RLY CO 1879
13 CH D 268, 28 WR 173, 41 LT 429, CA

NORWICH CORP v BROWN 1883
48 LT 898

OCEAN ESTATES LTD v PINDER 1969
2 AC 19, 1969 2 WLR 1359. 113 SOL JO 71, PC

OFULUE & ANOTHER v BOSSERT 2008
EWCA CIV 7

OFULUE & ANOTHER v BOSSERT 2009
UKHL 16 WLR (D) 91

OWEN v DE BEAUVOIR 1847
16 M & W 547

PARADISE BEACH & TRANSPORTATION CO LTD v PRICE
ROBINSON 1968
AC 1072, 1968 1 ALL ER 530, 1968 2 WLR 873, 112 SOL JO
113, PC

PAVLEDES v RYESBRIDGE PROPERTIES LTD 1989
58 P & CR 459

PECO ARTS INC v HAZLITT GALLERY LTD 1983
3 ALL ER 193, 1983 1 WLR 1315, 127 SOL JO 806

PEMBERTONE v SOUTHARK LONDON BOROUGH
COUNCIL 2000   3
ALL ER 924, 2000 1 WLR 1672, 2000 2 EGLR 33, 2000 21 EG
135, 2000 EGCS 56, CA

PERRY v CLISSOLD 1907
AC 73, 76 LJPC 19, 95 LT 890, 23 TLR 232

POWELL v MCFARLANE 1977
38 P & CR 452

PRUDENTIAL ASSURANCE CO LTD v WATERLOO REAL
ESTATE INC 1999
2 EGLR 85, 1999 17 EG 131, 1999 EGCS 10, CA

PYE (JA) OXFORD LTD v GRAHAM 2000
CH 676, 2000 3 WLR 242, 81 P & CR 177, 2000 2 EGLR 137,
2000 07 LS GAZ R 42, 2000 08 LS GAZ R 36, 2000 EGCS 21,
144 SOL JO LB 107; REVSD SUB BOM PYE

JA OXFORD LTD V GRAHAM 2001 EWCA CIV 117, 2001 CH
804, 2001 2 WLR 1293, 82 P & CR 302, 2001 NPC 29, 2001 2
EGLR 69, 2001 18 EG 176. 145 SOL JO LB 38, 82 P & CR D1;
REVSD SUB NOM PYE JA

OXFORD LTD V GRAHAM 2002
UKHL 30 2002 3 ALL ER 865, 2002 3 WLR 221

PYE JA (OXFORD) LTD v UK 2007
APP 44302/02

R v ST PANCRAS ASSESSMENT COMMITTEE 1877
2 QBD 581 AT 588

R v SECRETARY OF STATE FOR THE ENVIRONMENT EX P
DAVIES 1990
61 P & CR 487

RAINS v BUXTON 1880
14 CH D 537, 49 LJ CH 473, 28 WR 954, 43 LT 88

RAMNARACE v LUTCHMAN 2001
1 WLR 1651, 2002 1 P & CR 371

RANDALL v STEVENS 1853
2 E & B 641, 23 LJQB 68, 18 JUR 128, 1 CLR 641, 21 LTOS 334

RED HOUSE FARMS THORNDON LTD v CATCHPOLE 1976
121 SOL JO 136, 1977 2 EGLR 125, 244 ESTATES GAZETTE
295, CA

RHODES v SMETHURST 1840
9 LJ EX 330, 4 JUR 702, A840 6 M & W 351, EX CH

RICHES v DPP 1973
2 ALL ER 925, 1973 1 WLR 1019, 117 SOL JO 585, CA

ROBERTS (MARK ANDREW) v CROWN ESTATES
COMMISSIONERS 2008
EWHC 513 CH 2007 2 P

ROBERTSON v BUTLER 1915
VLR 13

ROSENBERG v COOK 1881
8 QBD 162, 51 LJQB 170, 30 WR 344, CA

SEARBY v TOTTENHAM RLY CO 1868
LR 5 EQ 409

SECRETARY OF STATE FOR FOREIGN AND
COMMONWEALTH AFFAIRS v TOMLIN 1990
THE TIMES 4 DECEMBER 1990

SEDDON v SMITH 1877
36 LT 168, CA

SHELDON v OUTHWAITE LTD 1996
AC 102

SIMPSON v FERGUS 1999
79 P & CR 398, 79 P & CR D16, CA

SINDALL (WILLIAM) PLC v CAMBRIDGESHIRE COUNTY
COUNCIL 1994

3 ALL ER 932, 1994 1 WLR 1016, 92 LGR 121,
1993 NPC 82, CA

SMITH v LLOYD 1854
23 LJ EX 194, 9 EXCH 562, 2 WR 271, 2 CLR 1007,
22 LTOS 289

SMITH v STOCKS 1869
34 JP 181, 10 B & S 701, 38 LJQB 306, 17 WR 1135, 20 LT 740

SMITH v BENNETT 1874
30 LT 100

SOLLING v BROUGHTON 1893
AC 556, 63 LJPC 21, PC

ST JOHN v BOUGHTON 1838
9 SIM 219, 7 LJ CH 208, 2 JUR 413

ST LEONARDS v ASHBURNER 1870
21 LT 595

ST MARYLEBONE CO LTD v FAIRWHEATHER 1962
1 QB 498, 1961 3 ALL ER560, 1961 3 WLR 1083, 105 SOL JO
947, CA: AFFD SUB NOM FAIRWEATHER V ST MARYLRBONE
PROPERTY CO LTD 1963 AC 510, 1962 2 ALL ER 288, 1962 2
WLR 1020, 106 SOL JO 368, HL

STACEY v GARDNER 1994
CLY 568, CA

STACKPOOLE v STACKPOOLE 1843
6 I EQ R 18, 2 CON & LAW 489, 4 DR & WAR 320

SURRENDRA OVERSEAS LTD v GOVERNMENT OF SRI
LANKA 1977
2 ALL ER 481, 1977 1 WLR 565, 1977 1 LLYODS REP 653, 121
SOL JO 13

TAYLOR v LAWRENCE 2001
EWCA CIV 119, 2001 ALL ER D 180 JAN

TECBILD LTD v CHAMBERLAND 1969
20 P & CR 633, CA

THEW v WINGATE 1862
34 JP 183N 10 B & S 714, 38 LJQB 310N

THOMAS v THOMAS 1855
2 K & J 79, 25 LJ CH 159, 1 JUR NS 1160, 4 WR 135, 69 ER 701

THORNTON v FRANCE 1897
2 QB 143, 66 LJQB 705, 46 WR 56, 77 LT 38, CA

TINKER v RODWELL 1893
8 R 1, 69 LT 591, 9 TLR 657

TRELOAR v NUTE 1977
1 ALL ER 230, 1976 1 WLR 1295, 33 P & CR 41, 120 SOL JO
590, CA

TYRWHITT v WYNNE 1819
2 B & ALB 554

VANE v VANE 1873
8CH APP 383

WALKER v RUSSELL 1966
53 DLR 2D 509

WALLIS'S CAYTON BAY HOLIDAY CAMP LTD v SHELL-MEX
& BP LTD 1975
QB 94, 1974 3 ALL ER 575, 1974 3 WLR 387, 29 P & CR 214,
118 SOL JO 680 CA

WARD v CARTAR 1865
LR 1 EQ 29, 35 BEAV 171

WARREN v YOELL 1944
1 DLR 118

WARSAW v CHICAGO METALIC CEILINGS INC 1985
INC 35 CAL 3D 564 1985

WEST BANK ESTATES LTD v ARTHUR 1967
1 AC 665, 1966 3 WLR 750, 110 SOL JO 602, 11 WIR 220, PC

WESTMINSTER CITY COUNCIL v TOMLIN 1989
1 WLR 1287 CA

WIBBERLEY (ALAN) BUILDING LTD v INSLEY 1999
2 ALL ER 897, 1999 1 WLR 894, 78 P * CR 327, 1999 2 EGLR
89, 1999 21 LS GAZ R 39, 1999 24 EG 160, 1999 EGCS 66, 143
SOL JO LB 146, 78 P & CR D19, HL

WILLIAMS v USHERWOOD 1983
45 P & CR 235, CA

WILLIAMS BROS DIRECT SUPPLY LTD v RAFERTY 1958
1 QB 159, 1975 3 ALL ER 593, 1975 3 WLR 931, 101 SOL JO
921, CA

WILSON v MARTINS EXECUTORS 1993
1 EGLR 178, 1993 24 EG 119, CA

WIMPEY (GEORGE) & CO v SOHN 1976
CH 487, 1966 1 ALL ER 232, 1966 2 WLR 414, 110 SOL JO 15,
197 ESTATES GAZETTE 77, CA

WINDER v NA 1877
6 CH D 696, 46 LJ CH 572, 25 WR 768

WORSSAM v VANDENBRANDE 1868
17 WR 53

ADVERSE POSSESSION – STATUTE REFERENCES

ACCESS TO NEIGHBOURING LAND ACT 1992
ATOMIC ENERGY ACT 1946
CIVIL PROCEDURE RULES 2008
CIVIL PROCEDURES RULES 1998
COUNTY COURTS ACT 1984
COUNTY COURTS ACT 1984
CRIMINAL JUSTICE ACT & PUBLIC ORDER ACT 1994
CRIMINAL LAW ACT 1977
CROWN SUITS ACT 1769
CROWN SUITS ACT 1861
ELECTRICITY ACT 1989
GAS ACT 1986
HOUSING ACT 1988
HOUSING ACT 1988
HUMAN RIGHTS ACT 1998
INTERPRETATION ACT 1978
LAND CLAUSES CONSOLIDATION ACT 1845
LAND REGISTER (SCOTLAND) ACT 1979
LAND REGISTRATION ACT 2002
LAND REGISTRATION ACT 1925
LAND REGISTRATION ACT 1862
LAND TRANSFER ACT 1875
LAW OF PROPERTY ACT 1925
LIMITATION (NORTHERN IRELAND) ORDER 1989
LIMITATION ACT 1980
LIMITATION ACT 1939
LIMITATION ACT (STATUTE OF JAMES) 1623
LIMITATIONS (ENEMIES AND WAR PRISONERS) ACT 1945

LIMITATIONS ACT (STATUTE OF KING JAMES) 1623
LOCAL GOVERNMENT FINANCE ACT 1992
LOCAL GOVERNMENT FINANCE ACT 1992
MENTAL HEALTH ACT 1983
PRESCRIPTION AND LIMITATION (SCOTLAND) ACT 1973
PETROLEUM PRODUCTION ACT 1934
PROTECTION OF EVICTION ACT 1977
PUBLIC HEALTH ACT 1936
REAL PROPERTY LIMITATION ACT (THE LIMITATION ACT)
1833
REAL PROPERTY LIMITATION ACT 1874
WATER INDUSTRY ACT 1991

ADVERSE POSSESSION – ADDITIONAL REFERENCES

ADVERSE POSSESSION, S JOURDAN, BUTTERWORTH'S
LEXISNEXIS 2003 ISBN 0 40698251 1   2003

ADVISORY SERVICE FOR SQUATTERS (ASS) SQUATTERS
HANDBOOK, 12TH EDITION   2004

CIVIL PROCEDURES RULES SCH 1 46.2 (A) SCH 2   as at1948

CIVIL PROCEDURES RULES (PART 55)
(AMENDED 2008)   1998

COUNTY COURTS PRACTICE ORDER 26 RULE 5   as at1948

EUROPEAN CONVENTION FOR THE PROTECTION OF
HUMAN RIGHTS AND FUNDAMENTAL FREEDOMS (ECHR)
FIRST PROTOCOL ARTICLE ONE (UK RATIFICATION OF
TREATY 1953)   1953

FIFTH INTERIM REPORT OF THE LAW REVISION
COMMITTEE   1963

FIRST REPORT OF THE COMMISSIONERS ON THE LAW OF
REAL PROPERTY   1829

HANSARD OFFICIAL (UK PARLIAMENT) REPORT 3RD
SERIES COL 328 26 MARCH   1874

LAW COMMISSION AND THE HM LAND REGISTRY LAND
REGISTRATION FOR THE 21ST CENTURY A
CONVEYANCING REVOLUTION LAW COMMISSION NO 271
PARAGRAPH 10.4 & 2.72   1998

LAW COMMISSION REPORT ON LIMITATION OF
ACTIONS   2001

LAW REFORMS COMMITTEES 21ST REPORT ON THE FINAL
LIMITATION OF ACTIONS CMND 6923 PARAGRAPH
2.65   1977

RUOFF AND ROPER REGISTER CONVEYANCING LOOSE
LEAF EDITION PARAGRAPH 6 - 14   2000

TWENTY FIRST REPORT OF THE LAW REFORM
COMMITTEE   1936

UNITED NATIONS - CENTRE FOR HUMAN SETTLEMENTS
FOR THE DEVELOPMENT OF LAND REGISTRATION AND
LAND INFORMATION IN THE DEVELOPING COUNTRIES
(UNCHS NAIROBI)   1990

Lightning Source UK Ltd.
Milton Keynes UK
UKOW02f0032041116
286854UK00001B/27/P